The Enneagram Triads

A Key to Personal and Professional Growth

DICK WRIGHT

Molysdatur Publications
Novato, CA

Editor: Karla Huebner

Cover Design: Gary Head

Interior Design: Gary Head

Layout Production: Mike King Digital Prepress Services

Molysdatur Publications, Novato, California

Library of Congress Cataloging-in-Publication Data

Wright, Dick
The Enneagram Triads:
A key to personal and professional growth
p. cm.
Includes Index, Notes and Sources Utilized.

ISBN 1-882042-16-6: $14.95

Printed in the United States of America

01 00 99 98 97 96   5 4 3 2 1

Contents

List of Illustrations

Charts

Figures

Acknowledgements

I am principally indebted to Suzanne Zuercher, O.S.B., a
fellow 234 and friend of almost 30 years. Many of the
ideas contained within this book trace their way back to
her either directly or indirectly. It was Suzanne who
introduced me to the Enneagram by way of a series of
workshops she was conducting in the late 1980s. She
then generously shared her insights on the Enneagram
during two years of almost monthly tutorials, each lasting
several hours, and more recently through a number of less
frequent discussions. Our conversations, in addition to
providing me with a rich background, eventually chan-
neled themselves into the development of our
co-authored *Enneagram Cards*.[1] These were designed as
an unique instrument whereby people could tell their
own Enneagram story and thus identify first their
Enneagram triad and then their Enneagram type. Both
Suzanne and her brother, Jack Zuercher, S.J., have provid-

ed insightful editorial comment on the manuscript of this book.

I am also grateful to Paul V. Robb, S.J., who in the early seventies attended the first workshop on the Enneagram given at Loyola University of Chicago by Robert Ochs, S.J., who, together with Helen Palmer and Kathleen Riordan Speeth, had just attended Claudio Naranjo's first Enneagram workshop. Paul, a "resident" 567, has been generous in providing me his written Enneagram notes and his own keen insights into the Enneagram during many hours of one-on-one discussions. It was Paul who introduced me to Kenneth Walker's book, *A Study of Gurdjieff's Teaching*, cited in Chapters 1 and 3, which I found most enlightening. This book formed the basis of Paul's and Suzanne's approach to the Enneagram triads, which I have termed the Third Approach.

I am very thankful to Loretta Brady, Enneagram author, teacher, and therapist, who has encouraged me in this undertaking and has shared a number of her insights with me, particularly about her 567 "resident expertise." Spending hours pouring over this manuscript, she provided a wealth of penetrating editorial comment for which I am most appreciative.

I thank my business partner, John Elson, who as an 891 with many 234 characteristics provided living proof that one should not rely on external behavior alone when drawing conclusions about a person's Enneagram type. He has come to enthusiastically support my efforts to weave the Enneagram into our corporate workshops and consultations.

My special thanks to Andrea Isaacs and Jack Labanauskas, editors of the *Enneagram Monthly,* who published my series of four articles, the seed of this book. They graciously saw fit to put my first article on the first page of their first issue, for which I will ever be appreciative.

I have been touched by those who have attended my Enneagram classes, and especially by those in my ongoing discussion groups who in speaking about "how it is with them" have given me countless insights into the inner dynamics of each of the Enneagram triads and types.

Finally, I am especially grateful to my wife, Pat, who is conversant with the Enneagram and a "resident expert" in the 891 triad. She has kept my feet on the ground throughout my "Enneagram life" (as well as the rest of my life) and continues to provide me with down-to-earth insights into the inner life of 891s.

The
Enneagram Triads

A Key to Personal and Professional Growth

Introduction

In coming to terms with the human experience, it is important to grasp the basics before moving on to complexities. In this book I present what I consider the basics of the Enneagram personality system— the three "triads." Referred to by some authors as the three centers, the triads provide a natural starting point in approaching and comprehending the Enneagram personality system. Becoming acquainted with the characteristics, what I term the life stance, of each of the triads helps us begin to make sense of our experience of everyday life.

A word on the triads. Each of the three triads contains three of the nine Enneagram types. Throughout the book I shall discuss the triads in a certain order. The first triad I discuss is comprised of types Two, Three, and Four. For simplicity sake, I shall refer to this triad as the 234s. The second triad is comprised of types Five, Six, and Seven which I shall refer to as the 567s. The third triad is comprised of types Eight, Nine, and One which I shall refer to as the 891s. As I explain, the theme of each triad centers around one of the three Universal Functions *most accessible* to us: Doing for 234s, Perceiving for 567s, and Feeling for 891s.

The characteristics we share with others in our triad provide the basic underpinnings of our personality. Thus I believe the natural first step in our Enneagran journey is to determine our "resident" triad. Once we have identified our "resident" triad, we are, I believe, better equipped to move on to the complexity of identifying our Enneagram type.[1]

Why this book?

This book is based on the way I was taught the Enneagram and the way I have been teaching it since 1990. My purpose is to present a description of the three triads that is in keeping with both my own experience and that of many others who have been introduced to what I term the Third Approach. My description of the triads is also, as it turns out, in keeping with what I have come to believe was the approach of George Gurdjieff. He is the man credited with applying the Enneagram to the study of personality.

I believe that the triads provide a most insightful way of getting acquainted with the Enneagram. A study of the triads gives an initial taste of what the three different approaches to life are all about. This book is therefore an attempt to complement existing literature on the Enneagram by centering on the richness of the triads.

As I look back over my first experience learning about the Enneagram, I am thankful that I was introduced to it via the three triads. Initially I gained a grasp of which triad seemed to fit me. Then I moved on to explore the subtle nuances of the three types within that triad in order to identify my own type. Later I explored the other two triads. To this day, I continue to find exploration of the triads replete with insight.

My experience studying and teaching the Enneagram personality system has led me to three conclusions. First, the Enneagram triads (called "centers" by some authors) are the most underrated aspect of the system. Few authors take the time to explore the triads for more than a few pages. Rather, they prefer to focus on differentiating the nine Enneagram types.[2]

My second conclusion has to do with the shorthand phrase, "head, heart, and gut." While correctly capturing the inner dynamics of one of the three triads (the 567s), it somewhat misses the mark with the 891s and completely misses the mark with the 234s! There is agreement in Enneagram lore that "head" captures the center of activity for the 567 triad. "Gut" serves somewhat as a description of the 891 triad, but only in the sense of gut feelings. There is, however, a much more compelling anatomical descriptor of 891s that appears to have a solid historical grounding in Enneagram lore (see Chapter 3). The real misconception, in my view, arises with the characterization of 234s as the "heart" triad. "Heart" is the furthest thing from the *inner experience* of the 234 triad. 234s are the people most out of touch with their heart and what the heart symbolizes, feelings! Over the years, the description of 234s as "heart" or "feeling" people simply has not rung true to me as a "residing member" of this triad. What this book offers, perhaps more than anything else, is a fresh perspective on the 234 triad.

My third conclusion is that what an "outsider" perceives and concludes about someone of another Enneagram type can be very different from the "insider's" experience of self. Outsider attempts to accurately describe what may be going on inside someone else can easily lead to inaccuracies and errors in typing. And it is the description of what is going on inside, not necessarily a person's external behavior, that most accurately captures the personality of that individual. For instance, 567s can appear to be so knowledgeable, yet oftentimes they are panic-stricken inside. In actuality, they are desperately searching for an answer they haven't yet found. Likewise, 234s may appear emotional, but as skilled imitators, they have learned to act the part. Frequently their emotion comes not from deep inside, but is an outward presentation of what they deem appropriate to the situation. Finally, 891s often appear so strong, so tough. Yet inside they carry a very real feeling of their own vulnerability. Their strong feelings, if fully expressed, could cause them to lose control over themselves. This could result in their relinquishing control over themselves to others.

Each triad serves as a theme upon which three variations are superimposed. These variations, or subtle manifestations of each triad, are the nine Enneagram types. This book details the essential characteristics that comprise the "theme" of each of the triads.

Chapter 1 presents an introduction to what I term the Third Approach to the triads and discusses the historical foundations. Chapter 2 introduces the three experientially different life stances assumed by people in each of the triads. It introduces the three Universal Functions as well as three caricatures depicting the life stances of the three triads. Chapter 3 then presents an overview of the triads, comparing and contrasting them on a number of key characteristics.

Chapters 4, 5, and 6 expand on the key triad characteristics primarily by differentiating the ways in which the three types within each triad embody those characteristics. Chapter 4 deals with the 234s, Chapter 5 the 567s, and Chapter 6 the 891s.

Chapter 7 introduces the concept of the Clockwise Walk. This concept is integral to developing what I call internal and external applications of the Third Approach. Chapter 8 describes similarities in approach to life of the three "positions" within each triad: the first position (258s), the second position (369s), and the third position (147s). The Clockwise Walk accounts for a significant part of the dynamics connecting the Enneagram types in each of these three positions. Chapter 9 ends the book by discussing key strategies for relating to people in each of the triads.

This book can be read profitably both by those new to the Enneagram and those already familiar with it. I believe that those of you new to the Enneagram will find exploring the triads a much easier way to begin to comprehend the richness of the Enneagram than if you were first presented with the nine types. It is easier to differentiate between three than nine!

Those of you already familiar with the Enneagram will have an opportunity to step back and—perhaps for the first time—take a long look at the three very different life stances depicted by the triads. You will be able to compare the descriptions presented here with existing characterizations of the triads. The description of the 891s given here differs somewhat from the existing literature, while that of the 234s differs significantly. It is up to you to decide which description is truer to your own personal experience. This applies both to the description of your own "resident triad" and to the "resident triads" of those with whom you are acquainted. Approaching this and any other Enneagram book with an open mind can lead to insights which deepen your own journey toward greater self-awareness.

CHAPTER ONE

A Third Approach to the Triads

THE ENNEAGRAM IS FIRST AND FOREMOST AN INNER WORK. It captures one's inner dynamics, the motivations behind one's behavior. It answers the question *"Why am I acting the way I am?"* Helen Palmer points out that the first reason to study typology is to "develop a working relationship with yourself." She goes on to say that the second reason "is so that you can understand other people as they are to themselves, rather than as you see them from your own point of view."[1] My attempt in the following pages is to describe people in the three triads "as they are to themselves," and not necessarily as they may appear to others.

The need to focus on the inner rather than the outer was vividly expressed during a workshop I attended a few years ago. "Don't judge a book by its cover," a person in the 567 triad exclaimed when asked what advice he would give to others in dealing with 5s. "There is more inside than I would ever be comfortable letting you know." Don't judge the inner by the outer!

Enneagram authors tend to follow one of two classic approaches to describing the three triads. The first and most popular approach is the "Head/Heart/Gut" characterization, a specific application of which is presented by Helen Palmer in her book, *The Enneagram.* Speaking about the three ways individuals can "focus attention," she identifies "those with mentally-based intuitions, those with feeling-based intuitions and those with gut or body-based intuitions."[2]

A second approach, presented by Don Riso, moves beyond the "Head/Heart/Gut" characterization which he, for some reason, labels as "Jesuit teaching."[3] According to Riso, one type within each triad overdevelops the "characteristic faculty" of that triad, another type underdevelops its faculty, while the third type is most out of touch with the faculty. Riso terms the 234s "The Feeling Triad," the 567s "The Doing Triad," and the 891s "The Relating [to the Environment] Triad."[4] In effect, Riso identifies the triads by that faculty which each triad has the most difficulty with.

There is, however, a Third Approach to describing the triads or centers, that presented by Paul Robb and Suzanne Zuercher.[5] This approach characterizes each triad by the function that instinctively takes hold of people within the triad, in other words, by the function that comes naturally. In this approach 234s are called the *Doers,* 567s the *Perceivers,* and 891s the *Feelers.*

Bear in mind that all three of these Universal Functions—doing, perceiving, and feeling—are present in each of the triads. However, for people in each triad, one of these functions is Instinctive, another is Auxiliary, and the third is Buried. The lifetime challenge of self-awareness, coming to the realization of "how it is with me," involves opening oneself up to and touching into all three of these Universal Functions.

I approach this exploration of what I believe is a more true-to-experience description of the three triads in the spirit of openness proposed by Don Riso.

Since it is probably impossible to find the original source of the enneagram, we are free to approach each modern interpretation as a separate point of view on this remarkably rich symbol. All may not be equally valid (indeed, all cannot be), but all have a right to be heard.[6]

A comparison of the three approaches is found in Chart 1.

Chart 1
The Triads: Three Approaches

Triad	First	Second	Third
234	Heart	Feeling	Doing
567	Head	Doing	Perceiving
891	Gut	Relating	Feeling

Why do I favor this Third Approach? For two reasons. First, and most important, I have found the descriptions of what the triads "do best" more intuitively appealing and truer to my own experience. I have seen this played out over and again during years of teaching this approach to students in my corporate and personal development workshops. Given this Third Approach presentation, students have been able to identify their triad almost immediately and usually quite accurately. Second, I have come to believe that this Third Approach reflects Gurdjieff's teaching on the centers.[7]

The Historical Foundation

George Gurdjieff is the man credited with having applied the teachings of the Sufi mystics to the study of personality. Having returned to his native Russia from his wide-ranging travels, he began discussing his findings with a small number of pupils, one of whom was P.D. Ouspensky. Fascinated by what Gurdjieff had to say, Ouspensky remained a close colleague.

Ouspensky and Gurdjieff left Russia in 1917, during the Russian Revolution. They headed first for Constantinople and then eventually moved on to France, where Gurdjieff was to remain.

The decade from 1923 to 1933 was spent in intense work with students at the "Institute for the Harmonious Development of Man," during which time

Gurdjieff tested and revised a system of study, self-observation, physical work and exercise deemed toward the reconciliation and union of the three basic human functions of *thinking, feeling, and physical activity.*[8]

Shortly after arriving in France, Ouspensky was invited to England. There he remained for over thirty years teaching Gurdjieff's approach to personality.[9] In similar fashion, Gurdjieff's teaching began to be slowly and quietly disseminated beyond France. As Don Riso notes, "The Enneagram was subsequently transmitted, along with the rest of Gurdjieff's teachings, through small private study groups in London, New York, and around the world."[10]

I came to the belief that the Third Approach accurately reflects Gurdjieff's teaching after having read Kenneth Walker's discussion of the "Three Centres" in his little-known book, *A Study of Gurdjieff's Teaching* (London: Jonathan Cape, 1957).

Walker was a student of P.D. Ouspensky while the latter taught the Gurdjieff work in London. In addition to studying with Ouspensky, Walker travelled to Paris a number of times to meet and talk with Gurdjieff himself. So taken was Walker with Gurdjieff's teaching that he wrote two books, *Diagnosis of Man* (1942) and *A Study of Gurdjieff's Teaching* (1957). It is his second book that provides great insight into what I refer to as the triads.

In his preface to *A Study*, Walker writes:

The account of Gurdjieff's teaching contained in this book is very far from being complete. It was not my intention to give a full report of it, but to comment on those parts of his system of knowledge which have made a particularly deep impression on me or which I have felt to be of special importance.[11]

Walker clearly indicates that his knowledge of Gurdjieff's teaching came from Ouspensky.

I owe a great deal to Ouspensky for all he did for me in those earlier years, and I am deeply grateful to him for his patient and clear-headed interpretation of Gurdjieff's teaching. He had a much better command of English than did Gurdjieff and a methodical and tidy mind which imposed order on the latter's less systematized method of teaching....G and O are now dead and if I am ever to put on printed record what I learned from them it must be now.[12]

Gurdjieff, Ouspensky and the Three Men[13]

What did Walker have to say about the "Three Centres?" He writes that Ouspensky used as his starting point Gurdjieff's description of man as a "three storied being," each story containing a different "mind" or function.

In the top story there resided the intellectual mind, or, as Ouspensky preferred to call it, the Intellectual Centre. In the middle story was man's emotional mind or Centre, and in the lower story both his moving and his instinctive minds or Centres.[14]

Walker goes on to say that "the relative activity of the three chief centres in man [intellectual, emotional and moving/instinctive] was different in different individuals, and this provided us with a means of classifying men under three headings."[15]

This same division into emotional, intellectual, and moving centers is also reported by Kathleen Riordan Speeth, who together with Robert Ochs, S.J. and Helen Palmer, was one of Claudio Naranjo's first Enneagram students in the early 1970s. Citing Gurdjieff's three "stories," Speeth then differentiates the three types of man. Each of these "men" is characterized by a predisposition to function according to his predominant "brain"—what each person, in my terms, "does best."

The relative importance of an individual's patterns of functioning of each of the three stories [of his personality] determines his place in the scheme of classification used by Gurdjieff to characterize man. One person may depend more on his head than on his heart, for example, while another may allow emotion to sway him where logic fails. Everyone is born with one "brain" predisposed to dominate over the other two. According to Gurdjieff's scheme Man

Number One has his center of gravity in moving and instinctive functions, Man Number Two gives more weight to feelings, and Man Number Three bases his actions on his knowledge or theoretical perspective. These individuals are more or less on the same level of being, since they all lack inner unity and will. They differ, however, in their reliance on one function over another.[16]

Speeth goes on to describe Man Number One as "moving/instinctive man" who relies on imitative learning. Man Number Two is titled "emotional man" and is characterized by knowledge of likes and dislikes. Man Number Three is "thinking man" who relies on logical thinking and literal interpretations.

Speeth differs from the Third Approach as to which centers are represented by Man Number One and Man Number Two. However, her brief descriptions of the characteristics of the three types of persons provide insight into what I perceive to be the inner motivations of each of the three triads. The 234s I see as "moving/instinctive man," the 891s as "emotional man," and the 567s as "thinking man." Chapters 3 through 6 present my case for this characterization.

A comparative chart should clarify these three related viewpoints:

Walker's most significant insight concerns each of the triad's natural instincts.

There were men who did everything by *imitating* the behavior of those around them, and who thought,

Chart 2
Gurdjieff, Ouspensky, and Speeth

	Gurdjieff	Ouspensky	Speeth
Man #1	Moving Mind	Moving Function	Moving/ Instinctive Man
Man #2	Emotional Mind	Feeling Function	Emotional Man
Man #3	Intellectual Mind	Thinking Function	Thinking Man

felt, moved and reacted much as everybody else thought, felt, moved and reacted. Such people were controlled almost entirely by their *moving centres* which possessed a special gift for imitation, and a man of this type would then henceforth be referred to as Man Number One.

There were other people in whose lives the emotions played a leading part, people who were guided by what they felt and what they liked and disliked rather than by what they thought. Such people spent their lives in seeking what was pleasant and avoiding what was unpleasant, but sometimes they reacted pathologically in the reverse way, extracting a perverted pleasure from fear and suffering and converting what was distressing into a horrid form of voluptuousness. An emotionally controlled [which in this context means *driven*] person of this kind would be spoken of in future as Man Number Two.

Finally there was Man Number Three, the man who was swayed by theories and by what he called his reason, a man whose knowledge was based on logical thinking and who understood everything in a *literal sense.*[17]

We now have an historical basis for the description used in the Third Approach, *one presented by a man who studied for years with Ouspensky.* Walker has described the three triads in terms of what they are good at, what comes to them instinctively, and what predisposes them to view and respond to reality as they do. Walker, in effect, describes the triads by *what each does best!*

This delineation of the "Three Men" provides a perspective very different from that of the popular "Head/Heart/Gut" approach. As I show with the three caricatures in Chapter 2, the Third Approach identifies a distinctive anatomical center for each of the three triads which, as it turns out, is very consistent with Walker's account of Ouspensky's teaching.

I would suggest that Ouspensky's "Man Number One," the "imitator/mover/reactor," describes people in the 234 Triad (the *Doers*). "Man Number Two," whose "emotions play a leading part," seeking the pleasant and avoiding the unpleasant, describes people in the 891 triad (the *Feelers*). "Man Number Three," the "literal, logical theoretician," describes people in the 567 triad (the *Perceivers*). It is time now to turn to a description of these three functions together with a portrayal of the life stance of each of the three triads.

CHAPTER TWO

The Three Universal Functions

ATTEMPTING TO UNDERSTAND THE INNER DYNAMICS OF people in each of the three triads is a most rewarding experience. To do so using the Third Approach, it is important to get an accurate picture of the dynamics of each of the three triads, particularly from the inside out. This chapter addresses each of the triads, highlighting the key *inner dynamics* which the three Enneagram types within each triad share in common.

Having identified the three Universal Functions, *Doing, Perceiving, and Feeling,* we must keep in mind that no matter which triad we are in, we each can and do experience all three. The key is that people in different triads experience them *in a different way.* This difference, as articulated by Don Riso, is a difference in emphasis.

No matter which Triad the basic personality type is in, everyone has the ability to feel, do, and relate to

the environment. We become one of the nine personality types because our psychological development, beginning in childhood, has emphasized one
faculty over the remaining two. But this does not
mean that the remaining two faculties are not a part
of us. They are, and we are who we are because all
three faculties operate in an ever-changing balance
to produce our personality.[1]

One of these functions, our *Instinctive Function,* will
tend to override the other two in awareness as well as in
expression. Another function, our *Buried Function,* will be
the most deeply hidden. It often becomes accessible to
our awareness and expression by way of our *Auxiliary
Function.* Wholeness and balance are possible only when
we get in touch with each of our three functions. However, even when we become aware of and utilize our
Auxiliary and Buried Functions, we filter them through
our own organisms. The experience and expression of
these functions will differ from triad to triad and from
type to type within each triad. Each of the three functions merges into the totality of our organismic response
to ourselves and the world around us.

Thus, we must be alert to one of the traps we can fall
into when studying type theories. This is the temptation
to stereotype, to attempt to explain the complexity of
human nature in simplistic terms. Reality is complex and
so any theory that attempts to explain reality must take
the complexities into account.

Doing, Perceiving, and Feeling

Having introduced the three Universal Functions, it is important to clarify the meaning of Doing, Perceiving, and Feeling in the context of the Third Approach. We begin with Feeling, which the Third Approach assigns to a triad very different from the other two approaches. We then describe Doing, a function articulated in the mid-seventies by Speeth as "physical activity"[2] but which, as far as I can ascertain, was utilized as a triad descriptor only by Paul Robb and Suzanne Zuercher. Lastly, we describe Perceiving, the "head" function about which there is agreement in the three different approaches.

Since *feeling* is such an overused word, it may be helpful to distinguish between "feeling" and "sentiment." Feeling is the basic instinct of 891s, while sentiment is the imitative "show" of 234s. One dictionary defines feeling as:

the undifferentiated background of one's awareness considered apart from any identifiable sensation, perception, or thought—the overall quality of one's awareness especially as measured along a pleasant-ness-unpleasantness continuum....the resulting state marked by pleasure, pain, attraction, or repulsion....[3]

Sentiment, on the other hand:

suggests a larger intellectual element than does feeling, applying commonly to an emotion *inspired by an idea, often suggesting a refined or an affected feeling.*[4]

Feeling, as thus defined, is much more primitive than sentiment. Feelings arise spontaneously from deep within; sentiments are more surface, "skin deep" rather than "from the depths."

234s, although they may look feeling-centered to others, are, according to the Third Approach, the types *least in touch* with their feelings. It is not that 234s have no feelings. Rather, people in this triad have buried their feelings. The natural instinct of 234s is to imitate and respond to their environment. This instinct prompts them to *focus outside,* not inside. 234s tend to pick up feelings, thermostat-like, *from the outside.* Then they act them out in the way, for example, that an audience member begins to take on and act out the enthusiasm of a charismatic motivational speaker.

The urge to "do something," the Instinctive Function of 234s, propels them into action. *Doing,* like feeling, can mean many things. One can "make do," "do up," or "do without." Each of these phrases connotes *process.* The Doing of 234s, on the other hand, has nothing to do with process. Rather, for 234s Doing is:

> to perform...to finish; bring to completion...to cause; bring about...to exert...to deal with as required...to work at...to produce...to play the role of.[5]

These definitions connote production: either *getting it done or acting the part.* According to the Third Approach, both of these are natural instincts of 234s, arising from their Instinctive Function. Perceiving is the Auxiliary Function of people in this triad and Feeling their Buried Function.

Unlike 891s, who are prompted into action by the energy of their feelings, activity comes naturally to 234s whether or not they feel anything! However, in their need to respond to their environment, especially to the people in their environment, 234s sometimes put on a show of feelings. They are natural "imitators," as Ouspensky termed them.[6] People in this triad, in responding to their environment, sometimes act out the feeling they deem suitable. The characteristic skin deep sentiment of the types in this triad—*Sentimentality* for the 2s, *Enthusiasm* for the 3s, and *Romanticism* for the 4s—comes not from deep within, but rather from an affected response to their environment.

234s can and do get in touch with their own primitive feelings, which comprise their Buried Function. However, there is almost always a time lag involved. 234s experience true feelings, *but attend to them only after the fact*—sometimes a few moments later, sometimes years later! 234s need to reflect before they feel. They need to look back in thought, using their Auxiliary Function, Perceiving, before they begin to get in touch with what they truly felt in the past and before they can let themselves experience what they truly feel here and now.

891s, on the other hand, are closest to their primitive

feelings. Feeling is their Instinctive Function, Doing their Auxiliary Function, and Perceiving, or achieving perspective, their Buried Function. People in this triad, as described by the Third Approach, instinctively live life based on a *felt sense* of good or bad, right or wrong. This felt sense of right and wrong results in deeply felt convictions, and these convictions energize and direct the outlook and actions of 891s. Feeling for 891s translates immediately into a *judgment* about a situation, a person, or themselves. At any given moment things are either good or bad, right or wrong, pleasant or unpleasant.

Moved to action by their felt sense of right and wrong, the feelings of people in the 891 triad keep them stuck in the immediate present. At any given moment *they are their feelings*. Reflection, their Buried Function, is not necessary to get in touch with their feelings as it is with 234s. Reflection is, however, necessary to provide 891s with the wide-angle lens that can put their present feelings into perspective. Reflection helps 891s realize they are more than their feelings-of-the-moment. Only upon reflection can 891s begin to understand that the judgment they made so quickly and instinctively may not be accurate (although often it is). Only upon reflection can 891s learn to hold on to opposites, to break through their "either/or" outlook.

An analogy may help. Imagine leaving an air conditioned house and encountering the 100-degree temperature outside. 234s immediately would *feel the heat;* 891s immediately would *feel themselves hot.* After a time 234s would begin to feel themselves hot. After reflection, 891s would realize that feeling hot is temporary because they can go back inside the house and feel cool.

Feeling, the instinct of 891s, and sentiment, the imitative, affected display of 234s, are contrasted in Chart 3. Even 567s are closer to their primitive feelings than are 234s!

Chart 3

Feeling Versus Sentiment

Feeling (891s) is ...	Sentiment (234s) is ...
Instinctive	Constructed
Primitive	Superficial
Rising from deep within	A response to a situation
Genuine	Affected
A felt sense	An acting out
Experienced	Created and staged

According to the Third Approach, *Perceiving* is the natural instinct of 567s. The dictionary definition of Perceiving is:

> to become aware of through sight, hearing, touch, taste, or smell...to take hold of, comprehend...to grasp mentally, take note of, recognize, observe.[7]

This accurately describes the Instinctive Function of 567s. They desire to find a place of safety that protects them from a potentially chaotic and threatening world. To gain safety, people in this triad instinctively step back or at least hold back. Even if only for a moment, holding back allows them to observe everything they can, bring-

Chart 4
The Three Universal Functions

Triad	Instinctive Function	Auxiliary Function	Buried Function
234s	Doing	Perceiving	Feeling
567s	Perceiving	Feeling	Doing
891s	Feeling	Doing	Perceiving

ing them into the place of safety they find within. They are then free to process the data gathered from outside and gain perspective.

While aware of their primitive feelings, their Auxiliary Function, 567s tend to keep these feelings at arm's length. This is due to a strong suspicion that feelings will muddy the waters. Feelings can interfere with the dispassionate, disengaged processing of data. Furthermore, 567s know that feelings, once admitted, tend to prompt them to action. Even if action is nothing more than coming to a decision, taking action, Doing, is their least familiar and least safe function. It is their Buried Function. Chart 4 provides a summary of the three Universal Functions.

The Three Approaches to Life

I believe it is very important for those new to the Enneagram to focus first on which triad best represents their energy. This is a meaningful step to take before entering into the richness and complexity of the nine Enneagram types. I have found the following exercise to

Figure 1
The Three Caricatures

be an excellent initial way to sort out who we are. Even for those familiar with their types, the exercise can be eye-opening!

Figure 1 is the first exercise I present when introducing the Enneagram in my introductory workshops.[8] I ask participants to look at the three caricatures in Figure 1 one at a time. I urge them to ponder which one *most accurately* depicts who they are.

Bear in mind that as you view the three caricatures and read the brief descriptions of their differing "energy" you will likely see elements of yourself in all three. Human beings are complex, and in terms of the Enneagram we possess some characteristics from all three triads and all nine types. It is also true, however, that each of us is one type and, therefore, resides in only one of the three triads. So I ask you to look for what civil law terms "the preponderance of evidence." Which of the three figures *most accurately* depicts you and the focus of your energy?

Let us begin the process of identifying your "resident" triad. Think back to when you were a child, sometime during or before you entered grade school. The reason we look back at childhood is that as children we already attempted to create our personalities. We began to develop a working self-image that allowed us to live with ourselves as well as adjust to what we perceived as the demands and expectations of our parents and other significant people. As you look at each of the three figures, try to determine which most faithfully depicts who you were. You will likely see elements of yourself in all three, but chances are one will stand out more than the other two.

In the process of creating our working self-image, we tended to exaggerate certain aspects of ourselves and to minimalize, deny, or "forget" other aspects. These childhood distortions, exaggerations, and denials, Jolande Jacobi tells us, were our attempt to create the "loveable child," the person we could live with. They were also our response to the demands of the outer world.[9]

It is not as if one day we sat down with paper and pencil and drew a sketch of what we wanted to be. Our created self-image happened naturally, as a result of our underlying personality dynamics. For instance, when we listened to what our parents said, certain comments stood out more than others. While our parents most likely made and repeated other comments besides those that we remember, we filtered out what we did not want to hear. The remembered comments were probably more in keeping with the values and self-image linked to our personality type.

Look first at Figure 2. Immediately you will notice exaggerations and minimalizations. These children were always in motion and so the feet are exaggerated. Hands, also exaggerated, were for doing things once their feet got them there. The spinal column, which holds them together and keeps them active, is most pronounced. But notice there is no *inside*. At ease in the outer world where the action was, these children "forgot" their insides. Although the head is of somewhat normal size, the ears are exaggerated. Why would these children need ears? By listening, by picking up cues and clues from the people in their environment, these children came to understand what others wished and expected of them. Once they

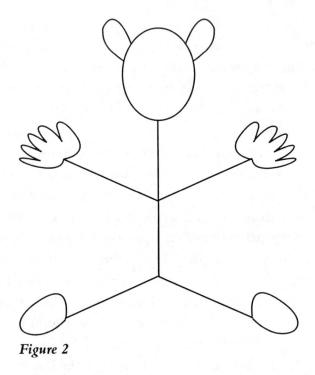

Figure 2

knew what was expected, or at least what they perceived was expected, these children had a mandate to action. Upon completion of any action, they needed their ears again. They needed to hear how well they had done. "How did I do, Mommy?" was always on their minds if not on their lips. Life to these children meant "doing" in the outer world and being noticed and rewarded for their actions.

Now look at Figure 3. Once again you will notice exaggerations and minimalizations. The most exaggerated feature is the very large head. Exaggerated within the head are the eyes. The rest of the body is almost nonexistent, certainly of less importance than the head.

Figure 3

These children noticed everything. Their eyes were wide, taking it all in. They were fearful of the outside world and felt ill at ease "out there." If they could take the outer world and bring it inside their heads, they began to feel safe. Safety came from standing apart from what was out there and sorting through the data. This was done in an attempt to figure out what it all meant. Outside was chaotic; inside was more tidy, orderly, and certainly more quiet. One person in this triad said that when she was young she used to enjoy standing behind the sofa when company came. From this vantage point she could watch the friends and relatives who came over to the house. Her parents never asked her to be part of the gathering. Indeed, she never really wanted to join it, but was fascinated observing everything that went on.

These children had many questions, questions adults sometimes could not answer. At times these children realized they observed more than their parents did. Imagine the child who believes that life is a matter of noticing things and trying to figure things out. Then this child comes to the realization that adults do not always notice what they themselves notice! Such children begin to realize that they may have to fend for themselves. Yet they know so little. Taken up with their quest for meaning, these children "forgot" the rest of their bodies.

Now turn your attention to Figure 4. Yet again we see an exaggeration/minimalization dynamic, but played out very differently than in Figures 2 and 3. The child in Figure 4 stood firm. The psychological energy is rooted, frozen, grounded. Indeed, it would be very difficult for a child who looked like this to move. Everything below the neck is exaggerated, while the head is almost nonexistent.

These children had a deeply felt sense of what was good or bad, right or wrong, for them. Knowing what they liked and disliked, they had deep feelings about the way things should be. Sometimes they were bullies, sometimes protectors. Can you imagine how afraid other children might be of a child who looked like this? Or imagine how safe other children would feel standing behind someone like this! Sometimes people called these children stubborn. They did not budge; they knew what

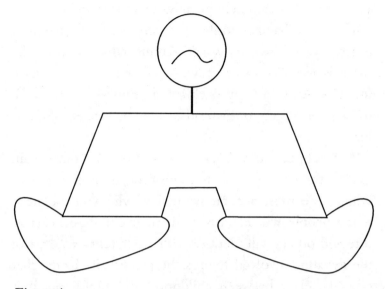

Figure 4

they wanted and what they did not want. They acted on their convictions. If they felt some activity was stupid, chances are they would not engage in it. On the other hand, if they thought something was of value, they probably became involved. These children "forgot" their head. Thinking and mulling things over was not important to them. Indeed, they had difficulty with those who spent so much time trying to figure things out. "What's there to figure out?" they wondered. "I know what I like" (the smile) or "what I don't like" (the frown).

Now that you have had a chance to look at all three figures, reflect a few moments and decide which one of the three most accurately depicts who you were as a child. What are your reasons for choosing this caricature? What is there about the caricature or its description that you feel most accurately portrays who you were?

If you are having trouble pinpointing the figure most descriptive of you, try to determine which one of the three is *least descriptive* of who you were. I often have found it helpful in approaching the Enneagram to work toward identifying one's triad or type by process of elimination.

At this point, come back to the present and once again look at the three caricatures. This time, think in terms of which one most accurately depicts who you are now. Some people will identify with their childhood caricature and others will identify with a different one. Part of the dynamic involved here is the process of change that can take place between childhood and adulthood. It is not that we have changed our basic Enneagram type. According to Enneagram theory, our types remain the same all our lives. However, our awareness and expression of our Auxiliary or Buried Functions may have changed. (There are other explanations of this dual identification involving the Enneagram concepts of wings and arrows which would take us far beyond the scope of this book.)

Figure 2 represents the 234 triad, the Doers. Figure 3 represents the 567 triad, the Perceivers. Figure 4 represents the 891 triad, the Feelers. You will recall from Chapter 1 that I believe Ouspensky's "Man Number One," the "imitator/mover/reactor," refers to the 234 triad; "Man Number Two," whose "emotions play a leading part," refers to the 891 triad; and "Man Number Three," the "literal, logical theoretician," refers to the 567 triad. It is time now to fill in the details.

CHAPTER THREE

The Three Triads: An Overview

NOW THAT WE HAVE SEEN AN OUTLINE OF EACH OF THE three triads, let us fill in the picture by comparing and contrasting their inner and outer dynamics. Chart 5 summarizes the characteristics we will cover in this chapter.

Instinctive, Auxiliary, and Buried Functions

As discussed in Chapter 2, each triad characteristically over-utilizes its Instinctive Function. This is the function people in the triad trust and rely on the most. Each triad is also able to tap into its Auxiliary Function, the next most familiar function. Each triad has a Buried Function. This is the most unfamiliar and least comfortable of the

Chart 5
Overview of the Three Triads

Characteristics	234s	567s	891s
Instinctive function	doing	perceiving	feeling
Trust their	actions	thoughts	judgments
Auxiliary function	perceiving	feeling	doing
Buried function	feeling	doing	perceiving
Stance toward life	move outward	hold back	hold ground
When compulsed	stay outside	stay inside	everything's either/or
When insensitive:			
to others	invasive	disengaged	brusk
to self	"I'm inadequate"	"I'm discounted"	"I'm weak"

When balanced	come inside	go outside	hold on to opposites
Search for	authenticity	truth	integrity
Need	connections	mental fit	boundaries
Automatically	make comparisons	seek answers	make judgments
Instinctive "center"	spinal column	head	solar plexus
life is a...	task to be done	riddle/mystery	struggle/battle/ hassle
		to be understood	
Conscious issue	image	meaning	vulnerability
Emotional issue	anxiety	fear	anger
Hooked by the...	future...	present...	past...
	behaviorally	perceptually	emotionally

three functions. Let us see how the three functions play out within each triad.

234s act first. Then they assess. Then they either keep up the good work or stop to modify their actions based on what they have observed. Their Auxiliary Function, perception, takes hold either in the midst of or shortly after the action they have undertaken. Perception as engaged in by 234s typically focuses on observing how others have reacted to them. Their observation is subjective, not objective. It serves as an aid in sorting through the cues and clues they pick up from others about how they are doing. Feeling, not part of their instinctive dynamic, is avoided or disregarded. It is contacted only if they are willing to let go by letting perception lead them into the realm of feeling, their Buried Function.

567s perceive first. Then they collect and sort their perceptions. From these they get a sense of what is important to continue examining or experiencing. They then discard what is not important to them and continue to pursue what is. Their observation is more objective than that of the 234s. For 567s feeling, their Auxiliary Function, becomes an aid in sifting through the data. It is touched upon either during observation or after the data have been collected. Action is not a part of their instinctive dynamic. It tends to be avoided or disregarded and is contacted only if they let go by letting their feelings take them into the realm of action, their Buried Function.

891s feel first and make an immediate judgment based on feeling. They then either act on their feelings or turn to something else. Action, their Auxiliary Function, is touched upon either in the midst of or shortly after the

feeling/judgment experience. Action flows naturally
when 891s feel strongly enough about something and it
serves as a natural release to their feelings. One of their
issues is *energy,* in terms of how much they have and how
they will expend it. Feelings tend to energize. When 891s
do not feel any energy inside, they look outside for
something to energize them. They seek to overcome
their boredom, to be stimulated. In effect, they *become*
feelings. Perception is not part of their instinctive
dynamic. It tends to be avoided or disregarded and is
contacted only if they let go by letting their action take
them into the realm of perception, their Buried Function.

The three Universal Functions, while available to each
triad, are experienced differently by people in each one.
"Doing" for 234s is simply and naturally taking up the
next task of life. For 891s, "doing" is acting on their feelings. It is their guide to gaining perspective. For 567s
"doing" is taking the risk of making a well thought out
decision and acting on it.

"Perceiving" for 234s is a moment of reflection *after the
fact,* whether on what they have just done or on what
someone else has just said. It is their guide to getting in
touch with their feelings. For 891s "perceiving" is widen-
ing their boundaries, opening themselves up to the grey
in life. "Perceiving" for 567s is the natural and instinctive
process of observing everything around them.

"Feeling" for 234s is initially the uncomfortable sensation of not being in charge, not being able to continue
doing. It is accessible to them as they become attuned to
their bodily sensations. For 891s, "feeling" is the natural

and instinctive body-based sense of what they like or dis-like. For 567s, "feeling" is what helps them sort through the data, guiding them into action.

Stance Toward Life

Each triad has a characteristic stance toward life, a posture that is both physical and psychological. This characteristic stance, which Paul Robb terms the "primitive, compulsive stance," comes instinctively to people in each of the triads. It is what they revert to when they feel cornered.

> 891s tend to shut down and to hold and stand their ground in a kind of lethargic "stuckness." 234s tend to move toward, to increase and intensify their goal-orientation....567s tend to withdraw, to spin dreams or theories, to gather data, to find explanations and excuses without attending to what is really going on.[1]

234s move outward into the arena of life in which they feel so responsible; 567s hold back and take in all the data they can. 891s hold their ground, careful not to be blindsided or to lose control of themselves to another.

Compulsion and Insensitivity

Compulsion, as used in this book, consists of overdoing what comes naturally. Each triad has its own compulsion issues.

234s stay outside of themselves when compulsed, engaging in even more activity. Their characteristic anxiety keeps them flailing around in accordance with the saying: "Having lost sight of my goal, I redoubled my efforts!" The more anxious they are, the more talkative or active they become. It is very difficult for 234s to "own" themselves as they are, apart from their actions. Compulsion can lead to *insensitivity,* literally the state of not being sensitive to others' needs or even to their own. When insensitive to others, 234s can become invasive, evasive, contemptuous, arrogant, vindictive, opportunistic, clinging, or exploitative. In one way or another they foist themselves into the lives of others whom they perceive as not appreciating (2s), respecting (3s), or understanding (4s) all they do. When insensitive to themselves, 234s put themselves down by saying "I'm inadequate," "I'm a failure," or "I don't measure up." All these putdowns refer to action taken or not taken.

567s stay inside when compulsed, engaging in even more observation and collection. Their characteristic fear brings them to a halt. When insensitive to others, 567s can become cold, distant, disengaged, delusional, paranoid, or dependent. They may then distort reality into what they impose on it rather than recognizing what it offers them. When insensitive to themselves, 567s think: "I'm of no account to others," "I'm overlooked," or "I'm discounted." All these putdowns refer to their perception of how others value their ideas.

891s move back and forth when compulsed, physically or psychologically enacting their characteristic "either/or" stance. They tend to focus on one thing at a time. This will be whatever consumes their current energy. They create boundaries between inner and outer, turning their backs to one at the expense of the other. Their bear-like "on or off" approach to life fixes them to this one piece of reality and to no other. When insensitive to others, 891s feel that "no one really cares," and can become brusk, harsh, abrasive, intolerant, passive, self-righteous, rigid, resistive, neglectful of self and others, punitive, or dogmatic. When insensitive to themselves, 891s, who identify so closely with their bodies, tend to feel "bad," "weak," or "power-less." All these putdowns refer to how they feel about themselves.

When Balanced, They Search for...

Balance, as used in this book, consists in opening oneself to the "whole" of who one is. It is learning to drop the exaggeration/minimalization dynamic and accept oneself as one really is.[2]

234s, when balanced, risk "coming home to themselves." This involves moving inward in spite of the fear that there "may not be anyone there." This movement within leads 234s on the road to *authenticity*. They begin to set aside their roles and titles and carefully crafted public images. They embrace the experience of self-as-I-am, not self-as-I-try-to-be.

567s, when balanced, take the risk of moving outside themselves. They share their insights with others. They take the leap of trust in themselves and in others despite the fear that they will be overlooked or discounted. This movement outside leads 567s on the road to a personally experienced *truth*. This truth is formed from the palpable, living reality found outside of their own minds.

891s, when balanced, take the risk of integrating opposites. This involves being open to the vulnerability that comes with facing the "grey" in life. This occurs despite the fear that they will lose control of themselves to another. Balance allows 891s to align themselves with the flow of life rather than getting caught up in the battle (8s), the struggle (1s), or the hassle (9s). It leads them to a personally experienced integrity, a state of being true to the self-in-its-wholeness, not merely to self-in-its-affect.

What They Need

234s need *connections* with other people. Afraid of what is inside, they need to feel at home outside, particularly with other people. They feel secure when they know they have a place in others' lives.

> All of these three types of persons [i.e. the 234s] consistently interpret the dangers that threaten them in terms of possible disconnection. Survival among these persons is based on a feeling of "social" security. They feel secure whenever they are accepted, liked by or connected to others.[3]

234s, as part of their connectedness to others, automatically make comparisons between themselves and others.

They strive to package themselves as more helpful than others (2s), better than anyone else (3s), more gracious than the rest (4s).

567s need *mental fit.* Instinctively curious, they want and strive to know how this new piece of data relates to all the data they previously have collected and sorted. Until they figure out how each new piece fits, they are uneasy and frustrated. They feel safe when it all fits together.

> For the Five-Six-Seven persons the greatest involvement is with their thoughts and ideas. They use the activity of the head to calm their fears. The focus of their energies is always on the need and desire to know. It's a matter of survival for them. They are seeking emotional and physical safety.[4]

567s in their quest for safety automatically seek answers to their questions. Some of these questions they may be hesitant to voice to others.

891s need *boundaries,* which help ensure self-preservation in their moment-to-moment existence. Very attuned to survival issues, they carve out their turf and work to keep themselves together. In striving to do so, at times they can exceed or blur their own boundaries. Nevertheless, they feel in control when the boundaries are clear.

> To all these three types of persons [891s] the dangers that threaten them in life are always interpreted as "survival" issues. The threat is that others may force

them to move against their wills. Only when these persons have a sense of being in charge of themselves, without control from others, do they feel secure.[5]

891s automatically make judgments, sometimes even before they are aware they have done so. This is one way of establishing those necessary boundaries between themselves and others and between what is good and bad.

Instinctive Centers

We all begin life from our true center. Ironically, in the attempt to grow up and become someone, we abandon our true center, our gut.[6] This abandonment takes the form of a *rising upwards*. People in each of the triads, abandoning their place of balance, pull upwards out of their true center to their instinctive center, the place from which they express their Instinctive Function. This instinctive center is used to "get on top of" their lives. In-corporating our essence, the instinctive center takes over and, if left to itself, can drive us into compulsion. Thus, in moving up from our true center we lose our balance. However, once we become aware of this preoccupation with the instinctive center, we can begin the process of regaining balance by coming back home to our true center.

For 234s, moving up out of the center takes them to their *spinal column*. In conjunction with their shoulders and rib cage, the spinal column forms an armor-like triangle that serves two purposes. It keeps others at a distance, preventing them from getting to the 234's feelings. It also keeps 234s standing on the alert, ever ready to produce, to be functional and separated from their deep feelings. 234s focus on production, getting things done no matter what the cost to themselves or others. Their instinctive center coordinates the movement and action of those arms and legs (Figure 2 in Chapter 2) which 234s rely on for their production.

567s, on the other hand, center all important activity in their *heads*. Taking in the data, seeing everything, taking things at face value, people in this triad have moved up to that place which allows them to observe from afar. The head is their place of inner control, that storage center which sorts the data, thereby keeping them safe.

The *solar plexus* is the instinctive center of the 891s who, even while thinking and acting so tough or so strong, are ever aware of their own vulnerability. The solar plexus is, after all, unprotected by the ribs, and while vulnerable if left unattended, can be tightened as a defense against harm. This is the very life posture of 891s: keeping firm, strong, and always on guard. The solar plexus also divides the body in half and thus symbolically captures the "either/or" stance of 891s.

Kenneth Walker provides the following description of Ouspensky's approach to the three anatomical centers.

When asked where, anatomically speaking these minds or coordinating centres of man were situated, he [Ouspensky] answered that they were widespread throughout the whole body, but that the maximum concentration of the intellectual centre [567s], or what could be called its centre of gravity, lay in the head. The centre of gravity of the emotional centre [891s] was in the solar plexus, and that of the moving centre [234s] in the spinal chord....Ouspensky advised that those of us that found this widespread diffusion of the various centres difficult to visualize should think of man's minds in terms of functions or activities rather than in terms of centres and anatomical structures. Instead of talking about centres they could say there were different functions in a man: those of thinking [567s], feeling [891s], and moving [234s] and that of regulating the various physiological needs of his body.[7]

Life Is a...

For 234s life is a *task* to be done. It is another project added to their endless list of activities, reassuring these "motion people" that they are getting somewhere. When balanced, 234s begin to experience life differently, as a given, as a process. It is no longer something to be worked hard for or achieved.

567s view life as a *problem* or *mystery* to be solved. It is a *riddle* to be understood, which continuously provides these "head people" plenty of data to be processed. When balanced, 567s begin to experience the fullness of themselves and of life. They see life differently, resonant with affect. It is no longer simply a collection of data to be analyzed or sorted through.

For 891s, life is about *energy,* whether or not to expend it in the battle, struggle, or hassle they continually face. Expending energy reinforces their need to be strong in order to stay in control. When balanced, 891s learn they can submit themselves to certain people or situations without being overwhelmed. They no longer judge life as something to be wrestled with (8s), avoided (9s), or purified (1s).

Conscious Issue

For 234s the issue is *image:* how do I look? How should I present myself? How am I coming across? What you see is what they want you to see.

For 567s the issue is *meaning:* I wonder what s/he meant when s/he said that? How does that fit in? What's it all about? They assume that what they see, you see.

For 891s the issue is *vulnerability:* getting through life relatively unscathed, expecting and putting up with "what happens." What you see is what you get.

Emotional Issue

The most familiar emotion for 234s is *anxiety,* which propels them into even more activity because they are not sure they have done enough. Their secondary emotion is fear and their least familiar emotion is anger.

For 567s the most familiar emotion is *fear*, which brings them to a grinding halt, afraid of the chaos that is lurking out there or within. Their secondary emotion is anger and their least familiar emotion is anxiety.

For 891s the familiar emotion is *anger* at a world that is not what it should be. Their anger either charges their batteries, propelling them into action (typical of 8s and 1s) or smolders inside while they work hard at staying calm (9s). Their secondary emotion is anxiety and their least familiar emotion is fear.

As with any of the Universal Functions, emotions are experienced differently by people in each of the triads. Each of us filters whatever we experience through our Instinctive Function. Since the filter is different, the experience is different. While we can empathize with others and attempt to understand what they might be experiencing, we can never truly experience things the way they do. The emotion of fear provides a good example of the differences in experience and expression.

891s with their instinctive reaction to real or perceived weakness, sense fear as a danger or threat which they take extreme measures to avoid; if caught in it, however, they stand firm. 567s with their instinctive reaction to real or perceived emptiness, shallowness, sense fear as overwhelming and so they shrink back and withdraw even before anything can happen. 234s with their instinctive reaction to real or perceived "not caring," sense fear as preventing their own "caring" and are propelled forward as if fear were always pursuing them. Just as 567s can stumble into reality in backing away, I wonder if 234s blunder into reality in being propelled forward.[8]

891s are afraid of being overwhelmed; they must stand on guard. 567s are afraid of the unknown; they must be prepared. 234s are afraid others will not care who they are, thereby undercutting their image and activity; they must keep busy.

Relationship to Time

The experience of time in our lives also varies according to our triad. Each of us, of course, experiences the three dimensions of time: past, present, and future. While all are available to us, we live differently in each of these dimensions. According to the Third Approach, one of these three time dimensions "hooks" us by way of our Instinctive Function. A second time dimension is the one in which we daydream or fantasize or play. The third is the one in which we tend to "forget" by ignoring or discounting.

234s are hooked behaviorally by the future. The future is where 234s really want to be because that is the focus of their helpfulness (2s), their success (3s), and their scripting (4s). *"What will I do next? What is the next item on my 'To-Do' list?"* Because they always are looking ahead, 234s usually do not see what is in the present. The present moment is a very thin line for 234s. They always seem to be trying to get to where they really want to be, the future. They tend to forget affectively in the present. They ignore and discount their feelings, which will only get in the way of their doing. When they get into the past, 234s dream perceptually by recoloring the past into the shades that most suit their current state.

567s are hooked perceptually by the present. The present is where they get stuck in their drive to observe and absorb everything. They dream behaviorally in the future, fantasizing about all the implications (5s), alternatives (6s), and possibilities (7s) open to them. They ruminate on what they might do. 567s forget the affect of the past. When they think about or narrate their own past history, they tend simply to recount the facts. They focus on the event rather than how they felt about it, reminiscent of Sergeant Joe Friday's "Just the facts, ma'am."

891s are hooked emotionally by the past. They are stuck in their undigested emotional experiences. These experiences may have arisen they know not when. Current encounters may catapult these emotional experiences into the present. Working very hard at simply getting through life, it is not easy for 891s to get out of the present and look toward the future. They forget perceptually in the future. They discount, ignore, or avoid what may come because of their need to get through the present, thereby losing the perspective that could free them from their "all or nothing" instinct. 891s dream behaviorally in the present. They sometimes act as if they are walking in a fog, unaware of the richness and variety of what is around them. They frequently lose or misplace things because their minds are either elsewhere or nowhere.

Reflecting on Your Triad

In my workshops, after presenting an overview of the triads, I ask participants to cluster in small groups with others in their triad to discuss the questions found in Chart 6.[9] You, the reader, might find it beneficial to spend some time reflecting on the questions of your triad.

Having compared and contrasted the three triads on a number of basic characteristics, it remains for us to examine each triad in more depth. Each of the next three chapters concentrates on one triad. Each chapter expands upon the basic triad characteristics by noting the three subtle variations in experience and expression demonstrated by each of the three "resident" types.

Chart 6
Triad Discussion Questions

234s

A. How does *image* play a part in your life?

B. What is it like for you to be *anxious*?

C. How is *getting things done* an important part of your life?

D. "How am I doing?" and "Who am I with?" are basic questions of this triad. What do they mean to you?

E. What helps you to *get in touch with the present moment?*

567s

A. How does *holding back* play a part in your life?

B. What is it like for you to be *fearful* or *apprehensive*?

C. What does *watching closely* mean to you?

D. "Do I belong here?" and "What's going on?" are basic questions of this triad. What do they mean to you?

E. What helps you *move outside yourself to take action*?

891s

A. How does *holding your ground* play a part in your life?

B. What is the experience of *anger* for you?

C. What is your experience of being guided by what you like or do not like in your life?

D. "Who am I?" and "Who has the power?" are basic questions of this triad. What do they mean to you?

E. What helps you to *stand back and gain perspective* in your life?

CHAPTER FOUR

234s: People of Production

THE BASIC INSTINCT OF 234s CENTERS AROUND DOING. People in this triad are Gurdjieff's "motion" people. Needing to be active, they approach life in accordance with Newton's First Law of Motion, "a body in motion tends to stay in motion." How accurately this law captures the dynamic of people in this triad! 234s are most comfortable and in touch with their *behavioral function:* accomplishing things, setting and achieving goals, undertaking projects; in fact, turning *everything* into a project. Time often becomes their enemy—so many things to accomplish and so little time! A person in this triad, after taking on a new position of wide ranging responsibilities, characteristically boasts after his first week on the job, "You just wouldn't believe all that I've accomplished in such a short period of time!" Doing is their Instinctive Function.

234s focus on what remains to be done. This is the first

meaning of the word "production" as applied to 234s. "Things To Do," either written on a list or playing in their minds, is an integral part of the dynamic of 234s, who see life as so many tasks to be accomplished. And, of course, once the task is accomplished, there is that delicious feeling that comes with crossing the item off the list. For 234s, this becomes the visible sign that they truly are "getting somewhere." Typically, that is all the reward 234s allow themselves, because they already are looking ahead to the next task. Convinced they have to earn their keep, people in this triad let their helpfulness (2s), achievements (3s), and the quality of their undertakings (4s) speak for themselves. They define who they are by what they do. Their written or mental "To-Do" lists keep 234s focused on the future. *"Are we there yet, mommy?"* Life to people in this triad is a series of destinations; the journey is secondary.

The stance of the 234s is *moving outward,* particularly toward other people, out into the arena of life where, to them, life itself is to be found. Because there is so much out there that takes up their effort and time, people in this triad are often uncomfortable with, unsure of, or afraid of the inner world. Finding themselves playing so many roles in life and playing some of them so very well, they fear looking inward because they are uncertain of who they really are. When they do look inward, they are apt to turn introspection into a project just as they make a project out of everything else in their lives. Their form of introspection is an anxious analysis akin to a grinding of gears not quite in alignment. It is a harsh, grating experience. They always are striving to make something happen so that time is not wasted. For example, 234s may be very disappointed if they conclude an introspective exercise without having achieved a result!

Connections with other people are very important. 234s often resemble telephone operators of the 1920s and 30s, moving plugs around the panel from one circuit to another, bringing a variety of people into contact with each other. 234s are linchpins, joining people to each other. This activity makes them feel good because they are "needed" (2s), "effective" (3s), or "appropriately engaged" (4s). However, people in this triad tend to focus so much on the connection that they sometimes forget there is a real person attached to the connection. A healthcare worker in this triad once commented, "I have to go take care of the broken leg in room 201." In focusing on his connection to the patient's needs, he ran the risk of being insensitive to the patient as a person. Centered on tasks and results, 234s often do not make the time or have the desire to get entangled with anything but the task at hand.

Relationships are indeed connections, but not all connections are relationships. A question of concern to 234s is "Who am I with?" They make sure they are part of the "in group" or they "network" in order to collect advantageous future contacts. These are ways by which 234s emphasize *image* and *usefulness.* Someone in this triad once commented, not altogether facetiously, "What good are friends if you can't use them?"

"How do I look?" "How am I doing?" "What do you think of me?" These are questions that 234s always have in mind even though they may not ask them aloud or in that way.

Instinctively trying to put their best foot forward, 234s do not want to be seen when they are not at their best. Walker, you will recall, reported that Ouspensky insightfully labelled people in this triad "imitators." 234s have an exceptionally fine-tuned ability to imitate *anything* others do. It is this ability which allows them to adapt to almost any circumstance. Their saccharine (2s), enthusiastic (3s), or dramatic (4s) show of feelings appears so real. *Appearance* is the key. It is sometimes just that: a show, a re-creation, an acting out of a response they learned to imitate from watching others. This is the second meaning of the word "production" as applied to 234s. Natural actors and actresses, 234s put on the show they think will play the best: what you see is what they want you to see! They would be mortified, angry, or embarrassed if you saw anything else.

> Instinctively social, 234 people adapt to what they think the environment and the people in it want of them. As a consequence, they may not even notice their own response to things, let alone their personal needs....They *look like* emotional people, either cheerful and friendly or heavy and melancholy. Actually, they have a hard time allowing into their experience and expressing to other people their emotional life. Emotions are pressed down, this is what "depression" means for them. The real emotional light of 2-3-4s seems to be missing because it is denied. Since it is missing they imitate what others feel and what the environment calls for.[1]

Creating an image combined with maintaining connections makes 234s experts in reaction-formation. This is the psychological defense mechanism by which one conceals or attempts to conceal one's real feelings from oneself and others, articulating to a person the exact opposite of what one feels about that person. For example, the less 234s like a person the more dramatically flattering, attentive, or complimentary they are. Wanting to be thought well of, 234s can maintain the semblance of a positive connection while in that person's presence, while revealing their real feelings to others after that person has left.

Because 234s play so many roles, they tend to struggle with *authenticity.* Roles, of course, are perfectly acceptable aspects of life as long as one does not identify so much with the role that one forgets who one really is. 234s are often at a loss as to who they really are. They tend to identify with whatever roles they are currently playing.

234s' emotional responses tend to be near the surface. Manufactured "sentiments" tend to replace feelings and can become substitutes for the real feelings with which 234s are so unfamiliar, uncomfortable, and inexperienced.

Feelings make themselves known to 234s in one of two ways. Either they result from something taking place in the outer world or they arise *after the fact* as reactions to an occurrence. A television documentary on the homeless, for example, may arouse in 2s an instantaneous burst of tears. Someone who puts obstacles in the 3's way, preventing completion of a project, may be the recipient of an angry outburst. A crying child may prompt 4s to call up memories of a long forgotten childhood hurt. Because 234s are so focused on the task at hand, feelings tend to be *discounted when they arise.* It is typically only after a time lag, after the feeling itself has come and gone, that a 234 can look back and say, for example, "You know, I was really angry!" People in this triad usually have to *name* their feelings in order to get in touch with them. Only then are they able to *let themselves* feel angry or hurt or afraid. Someone in this triad remarked that she usually sleeps on her feelings, especially her anger. If she feels the same way the next morning, then she realizes her feeling was genuine.

234s will know tomorrow what they feel today. It is not that 234s have no feelings. They *have* feelings, they *talk about* their feelings, they *analyze* their feelings. However, they do not easily *feel* them. 234s are simply *out of touch* with their feelings and therefore may not recognize them. They trust only their behavioral function and strongly suspect that feelings will derail them from what they need to get done. 234s are inexperienced with, unsure about, and ill at ease in the world of feelings. They don't know what to "do" with them! Feeling is their Buried Function.

Feelings energize and often prompt action. 234s, however, naturally act without feeling or at least have the need to *do something,* even though they may not be sure what. *Sentiment,* their manufactured feeling, can serve to initiate action on their part. 234s get in touch with their deeper feelings only when they can stop their doing and pause to reflect. Reflection for 234s allows their deep feelings to rise from within.

There is, however, one feeling with which people in this triad are very familiar—*anxiety.* It arises when "there is no need I can address" (2s), when they are not sure if they have "done enough" to be on top of things (3s), or perhaps have done something inappropriate or undignified (4s). Anxiety is that feeling of restlessness and incompleteness that prompts 234s to engage in even more action. Tapping their fingers is often a sign that they want you or themselves to "get on with it." For 234s, life is about getting on with things.

As experts on the outer world, people in this triad *take responsibility* for everything that comes into their world. *"If it is to be, it is up to me!"* 234s strive to be known as people who make a difference. They always are ready to give a response: a piece of advice (2s), a scheme (3s), a fitting remark (4s). Human thermostats, 234s are able to gauge the climate outside while unconcerned with what may be going on inside. They immediately respond to the situation as they read it.

234s seek *attention.* They want you to notice how helpful (2s), how efficient (3s), or how unique and special (4s) they are. They always are looking for clues as to what others think of them. 234s are apt to think well or badly of themselves based on the attention or feedback or reaction of others rather than on their own assessment of self.

234s tend to *compare themselves* to others. A teacher in this triad related that whenever a student praised another teacher in her presence she would immediately think,

"She's not as good as me!" For 2s the comparison takes the form of "I'm more helpful than...." 3s say to themselves "I'm better than...." For 4s it's "I'm different than...." 234s are elated if they feel they compare more favorably than the other and tend to think less of themselves if they feel they do not measure up.

As we have seen, feeling connected to others provides part of the security 234s need. They try very hard to make and keep the world around them secure. *"A place for everything and everything of mine in its place."* 234s actively arrange persons and things the way they want them to be. For example, gathering together all the necessary materials before beginning a project assures 234s they are in control of their world.

234s like to engage in tasks or projects that allow them to observe and continuously measure how they are doing. Their treadmill-like approach to life is so much more secure if the treadmill provides a running tally of miles covered, calories burned, time elapsed. Even process must deliver results! Measurement is one way 234s come to terms with process. A person in this triad, beginning to write an article, thought it would be more efficient to dictate her thoughts for someone else to type. She soon realized that dictation just was not working. She turned to the computer and began in a new way by typing her own thoughts. Soon she realized that typing, though not as efficient as dictation, was much more comfortable. It allowed her to monitor results and make on-the-spot adjustments. Dictation simply did not provide the continuous feedback she needed!

Compulsion, as introduced in Chapter 3, is simply overdoing what comes naturally. The compulsions of 234s, therefore, tend to center on activity in the outer world. When compulsed, 234s get *too close to others,* physically and emotionally invading, interfering with or imposing themselves on the lives of others. Getting close to others keeps the connections which are so important to 234s and which they fear losing. Getting close to others also keeps their focus on tasks and away from what is going on inside, that unfamiliar and therefore scary place.

Their challenge in achieving balance, however, is learning to *come inside* toward their true center. It will not help, though, if they try to do this in their customary task-oriented analytic way of picking everything apart. This inward movement will come gradually and only through periods of gentle reflection during which they quietly bend their minds back on their experience and calmly inquire of it. Most likely taking place while they are somehow in motion, this quiet reflection helps healthy 234s let themselves simply "be" without having to "do." This reflection, a form of Perception, is their Auxiliary Function.

CHAPTER FIVE

567s: People of Perception

WHILE THE DESCRIPTIONS OF THE INSTINCTIVE DYNAMICS of each triad yield much food for thought, we must remember that each of the three types within that triad experiences and manifests the underlying dynamic a bit differently.

> Because each type does focus on a particular dimension of the three hundred and sixty degree total reality, the types are likely to have developed a way of paying attention that is appropriate to their own concerns.[1]

The subtlety of those manifest differences is worth considering as we look at the various underlying dynamics of the 567 triad.[2]

According to the Third Approach, the instinctive function of 567s is *perceiving*. Their buried function is *doing*.

Their auxiliary function, which bridges the gap between Perceiving and Doing, is *feeling.*

> They [567s] learn best through seeing and are avid observers of their surroundings. The Fives stare, the Sixes take darting glances, and the Sevens quickly absorb everything in one smooth scan of delight. With all this mental activity they may seem to be without feelings. However, their feelings are very much alive and even accessible. It's just that they are hidden deep within them as safely buried treasure.[3]

Hooked perceptually by the present, people in this triad instinctively take *everything* in through their various senses. Human thermometers, 567s are acutely aware of and attempt to record all the data present in their environment. Convinced that there is more to life than meets the eye, they continually look beneath the surface. Noticing everything, they believe that others see the same things or see things the same way! It takes 567s a lifetime to come to understand that they notice more than many other people.

The stance of 567s is to *hold back* from anything in the outer world that is unpredictable, unexpected, and therefore scary. For 567s, experiencing life with all its unknowns is like entering a disco—smoke, noise, crowds of people, a rotating ball on the ceiling scattering specks of light all over the room—in other words, chaos, the very thing that 567s fear most! Their immediate reaction upon walking into that disco is to hold themselves back from the action.

5s physically hold back. They may move back against the far wall or into a corner where they can observe the whole panorama without being observed themselves. If they happen to be seated when they encounter someone or something new to them, they pull back into their chairs.

6s hold back from deciding and taking action. As they tentatively enter the disco, their eyes dart around in all directions. They are looking for someone to provide information on the rules of how to act. They hope this expert will be the next person they encounter.

7s hold back in a most unusual way. They override their hesitation by jumping into the unknown. 7s run from their fears while attempting to overwhelm the perceived threat with charm and distraction. This maneuver buys them time to collect new data without revealing any personal data that might suggest they are fearful.

The data collection process provides people in this triad something that is very important, *perspective*. 567s take in endless data from the outer world. They weave it with data from their own inner worlds, sorting and fitting everything into a personal jigsaw puzzle of life. When working a jigsaw puzzle, we need to bring order to the chaos of those many, many pieces piled in front of us. 567s instinctively do this by first looking for the boundary pieces that will begin to order the chaos of life. Only when they begin to control the pieces do people in this triad feel safe.

567s need to make a *"mental fit,"* relating how each piece of information fits with other pieces they have gathered. Their often unspoken but real question is:

"What does it all mean—what's it all about?" Other questions they have are: *"What's happening here?"* and *"How do I fit into it?"* or *"Do I even belong here?"*

The symbolic center of the 567s is the *head,* that place in which they feel safe and in which all of life's important activity takes place. Sponge-like, they fill their heads with all sorts of information picked up through their senses. As we saw in Figure 3, when caught up in the world of ideas, 567s can forget the rest of their bodies.

Life for people in this triad is a *riddle,* a *puzzle,* a *mystery* to be solved, a *problem* with a solution to be ferreted out. They collect things in order to resolve life's problems and to allay their fears. 5s collect data, 6s collect advice, and 7s collect experiences. The challenge and life work of 567s is a continual sorting, attempting to make sense of the world around them. Their issue is *meaning*—seeking to understand what is out there in their environment. Sometimes in the process of resolving the chaos they become overwhelmed by all the data collected. In this case, people in this triad may very well *impose* meaning on what is out there.

567s *seek answers.* 5s do this primarily on their own, either by using the research process or by turning questions over in their minds. When satisfactory answers emerge, the mental chaos settles into a meaningful pattern or system. 5s feel safe only if they understand what is going on.

6s tend to seek answers from others, asking anyone and everyone. Collecting volumes of possible answers, they may then seek advice on which answer is "most right." This process may go on indefinitely. However, if the fear of not knowing, of not being prepared, becomes intolerable, 6s may impulsively pick any answer just to end the mental confusion they are facing.

7s seek answers from others too, but in an indirect way, by engaging others in conversation and activity, picking the brains of those who have the data. This indirect process helps the hierarchy-conscious 7s keep themselves on an equal footing with others. During this activity, 7s pick up staggering amounts of information without ever being identified as questioners in search of answers. It then seems to others that 7s knew as much all along as those with whom they interacted.

Thus, people in this triad seek information in different ways, sure that the information will lead to truth. That search for truth—what is reality and what is not reality—is their most important quest.

567s' conscious emotion, underlying everything, is *fear:* fear of the unknown, the chaotic, fear of not knowing enough, not being prepared to handle a situation. Fear, unlike the anxiety that immediately prompts 234s into action, causes 567s to come to a dead stop until they *know enough* to take action.

Fear paralyzes the 5-6-7s, and causes them to stay in a safe, interior place arranging their gathered perceptions of the world and its people. They search for order inside that will protect them from threat outside and look for where they fit in the scheme of things.... Because fear paralyzes, actions do not flow naturally as the fruit of their perceptions.[4]

For 567s, courage means coming out of themselves. It can be something as simple as starting a conversation with a person they have just met (5s), trusting their own ideas and making a decision rather than relying on another's advice (6s), or openly expressing their fears while, for example, riding a mule down the rim of the Grand Canyon (7s).

567s have trouble with action and completion, with making decisions and acting upon them. After all, making a decision is the first action step. Since there is so much information out there yet to be uncovered (5s), because there are more people they could ask to confirm their ideas (6s), or because there are so many possibilities they prefer not to eliminate (7s), it may seem premature to make a decision. To decide this month, for instance, on which new car to purchase only to discover next month that it is the "lemon of the year" would mortify 567s; they would immediately blame themselves for not being thorough enough (5s), not asking enough people (6), or not test-driving enough different models (7s).

When 567s put themselves down they do so by thinking they are not interesting enough (5s), by convincing themselves that no one will pay attention to their ideas (6s), or by fearing that they have overlooked some vital alternative (7s).

Compulsion for 567s, as with everyone else, involves

overdoing what comes naturally. Thus, when compulsed, people in this triad *move even further inside* to that place of safety where no one else can touch them and from which they can observe from afar. They sometimes travel so far inside that they lose touch with reality.

Balance involves moving back to one's true center. For 567s balance means *moving outside*. This might involve taking the risk of revealing a part of themselves to others (5s), beginning to trust a specific person or situation (6s), or being willing to experience both the pain and the joy of life together (7s). They learn to share their insights and keen observations with others, discovering in the process that others can benefit greatly! They learn to trust and act on their feelings.

Their heightened ability to observe is what makes healthy 567s interesting enough for others to recognize and value them. They have a great deal to offer in terms of deep insight (5s), practical suggestions (6s), and creative synthesizing (7s). *They* must be the first ones not to overlook themselves or devalue their gifts. Learning to first trust themselves, they then can learn to trust others.

891s: People
of Passion

PEOPLE IN THE 891 TRIAD *FEEL STRONGLY* ABOUT THINGS. Feeling is their Instinctive Function. With 891s we encounter feeling in its deepest sense. This is a felt sense of what is good and bad, what they like and dislike, what is pleasant and unpleasant. Human seismographs, 891s register and are moved by deep sensations, thereby touching into the pulsating rhythms of life. Feelings, experienced by 891s throughout the body, quickly prompt judgments such as "I like it" or "I don't like it," "I want it" or "I don't want it," "I'm good" or "I'm bad." These judgments are articulated by people in this triad as *values*—what they hold dear and what they respect.

Rather than a mind set, 891s have a gut set. When this gut-knowing is translated to the mind in a logical argument, it is very hard to change. They get "locked in."[1]

Because they are so immersed in their feelings, 891s have trouble standing back in order to gain perspective. Perspective, their Buried Function, is difficult to achieve since a strong feeling has already prompted an almost instantaneous judgment. *"What more is there to think about or discuss?...I know!"* Experiencing nothing but where they are now, 891s exclude whatever is "not now" in their lives.

891s tend to focus their attention on *issues,* not on personalities. Those not in this triad often take the intensity of demeanor or the directness of the remark as a personal attack, but that is often not the 891's intent. It is the injustice or the wrongness in the *situation,* not necessarily the players involved, that triggers the 891's reaction. What to others may appear the prelude to a fight is often simply a statement, albeit heated, about the issue at hand.

People in this triad embody, as we have seen, an either/or approach to life: if it is not this, it must be that. Things, people, and situations are black or white, right or wrong, good or bad. It is all or nothing; there tends to be no middle ground. Thus, the psychological and often-times physical stance of 891s, depicted in Figure 4, is to hold their ground, to stand firm. It is vitally important for people in this triad to stand firm since they are motivated by such a deeply felt sense of right and wrong. Holding their ground manifests being true to themselves. When balanced, 891s become more comfortable holding on to opposites. They have then broken down the distinctions between either/or. They have learned to understand that life in its multitude of manifestations is neither black nor white but rather both. It is many "Shades Of Grey," as expressed in Billy Joel's insightful song.[2]

Integrity, acting on one's values, is very important to 891s. They become enraged when they encounter phoniness or lying, pragmatism or fence-straddling. They take exception to being manipulated, typically discounting flattery or what they feel are guilt trips. Responding directly out of their deep feelings, 891s' words, postures, and facial expressions "tell it like it is."

Vulnerability is an issue for 891s. Realizing how truly fragile life is and identifying so closely with their bodies, 891s are very much in touch with their own vulnerability. However, they will rarely let anyone glimpse this vulnerability, which they sense is a sign of weakness. Wanting attention, for example, they will not ask for it because to let others know they have a need leaves 891s vulnerable. Being strong, being in control, first and foremost of themselves and then of others, is one of their overriding concerns. Only after 891s become very close to and trusting of another might they be willing to display any hint of vulnerability.

Energy, whether kinetic or potential, is another issue for 891s, who tend to spend their energy only on what they feel is worthwhile. This is another manifestation of their value-motivation. Energy moves 891s toward Doing, their Auxiliary Function. If they think something is stupid, chances are they will not get involved. People in this triad become energized when they have a felt sense that they are right. How their energy is displayed, however, varies.

8s *kickstart* their energy, power-mower-like, which propels them into action. 9s *conserve* their energy. Because their concentration is so keen on keeping their environment peaceful, the 9's energy can be quickly dissipated. 1s *focus* their energy, laser-like, on removing the flaws they see all around them, both inside and outside.

People in this triad sense they have to take care of themselves. "No one ever took care of me; I'm responsible for myself," asserted a person in this triad. Later in the conversation she commented, "If people don't like me, it's their problem!" 891s pride themselves on their rugged, sometimes stubborn, self reliance. 891s, unlike 234s, do not seek or even need affirmation. They reinforce themselves.

891s instinctively sense that life entails taking one step at a time. Adjustments must be made here and now. The present moment is really all one has. Stuck in the inertia of the moment, people in this triad often become completely absorbed in whatever has their attention at the present time, to the exclusion of everything else. Once they turn to something else, that then will completely hold their attention.

891s typically experience life as a *struggle,* a *battle,* or, at the very least, a *hassle.* Their stance toward life is to hold their ground. 9s tend to experience life as a struggle: simply getting through it, avoiding or preventing conflict, staying calm, striving for harmony. The "battle stance" is more typical of 8s and 1s, the former battling against the oppressor, the latter battling for what is right. As a corporate executive (an 8) once acknowledged, "It's the fight that's important to me, not the victory!" The "hassle" is more typical of 9s and 1s. A 1 acknowledged: "Nothing worthwhile comes easily. You have to strive for everything you want."

People in this triad fear being blindsided, losing control, being swept away either by others or by their own strong feelings. As a result, they expend a great deal of energy keeping themselves or the situation under control. In this process 8s become enraged, 9s overwhelmed, and 1s resentful when they are not able to take control. The emotional issue is *anger.* 891s tend to turn their fears into anger either actively or passively. 8s and 1s actively use their anger to propel them into action, into the battle they expect will take place. 9s, on the other hand, passively sit on their anger, holding it down. 9s tend not to express anger for fear of losing control over themselves and thereby possibly giving control of themselves to others.

> The intense emotional response of 8-9-1s is what frightens them more than anyone else. The first person they feel they need to control is the one within. This they try to do by answering their own emotional response with reason and logic. Depending on the individual space among the three, 8-9-1s either consciously curb their emotions by an organized, rational defense or else fail altogether to be aware that they have strong feelings.[3]

Oscar Ichazo has identified two 891 questions: *"Who*

am I?" and *"Who has the power?"*[4] "Who am I?" has to do with boundaries, something people in this triad wrestle with. When dealing with an issue, 8s tend to expand far beyond their own personal boundaries. 1s typically contract in order to comply with the exacting standards they have internalized. 9s have a tendency to merge with a "significant other" whom they feel will support them. This way 9s instinctively blur the boundaries between self and other.

> When tides of emotions rise between themselves and others in relationships, 8-9-1s often find their own personal boundaries washed away. This experience is the other side of—and possibly the reason for—strong self-preservation instincts. Conservation of energy, of time, of involvement are attempts to keep their individual person from becoming merged with others. Where self and another begin and end becomes the issue in their emotion-laden existence, whether they are conscious or not of the depths of their affectivity.[5]

891s sense the *power* in a situation. They understand, for instance, that in an organization a title after one's name does not necessarily connote power. Power, like respect, must be *earned*. 891s quickly assess who can make things happen. In a school setting, for example, 891s know the janitor and the secretary can make things happen because the janitor has the keys and the secretary has unlimited access to the copy machine!

People in this triad get hooked emotionally by the *past*. They carry their strong feelings—their angers (8s), their bitter disappointments (9s), their resentments (1s)—from the past into the present, thereby coloring the present, just as a small drop of food coloring quickly permeates an entire glass of water. Somehow, often unconsciously, the situation or the person they are now facing reminds them of something or someone they encountered or experienced in the past. Depending on the feeling aroused, this may prompt either a positive or a negative reaction. 891s tend to think and speak in analogies, and sometimes that is how they and others come to realize what feelings they are carrying from the past into the present.

> Oftentimes when asked how they feel they will answer as saying; "It's like the time when I...". As you listen to this story from their past experience they seem to be saying that the feeling they had at this earlier time is somewhat similar to the way they feel now.[6]

Just as with people in the other triads, compulsion for 891s consists of overdoing what comes naturally. When compulsed, 891s overdo their vigilance in keeping themselves and others under control. They do this by *exaggerating the boundaries* between themselves and others. They remain ever on guard lest they be overwhelmed by hostile inner or outer forces. They divide the world into good and bad and get stuck in either/or.

When balanced, 891s have a down-to-earth, feet-on-the-ground, no-nonsense presence that can be very reassuring to others, particularly, I suspect, to 234s. This presence results from their being able to *reconcile opposites* in their lives: the good and the bad, the weak and the strong, the passion and the innocence. Boundaries can be set aside. One can be refreshingly honest and direct with healthy 891s. Their tough exterior protects the very vulnerable child within. Yet this tough exterior can be pierced with an honest comment about oneself or even about them, thus providing a moment or two of genuine human contact. Steady, persistent, determined, and anchored in their beliefs and values, healthy 891s deal with life head-on. Healthy 891s truly are "passionately engaged" with life!

CHAPTER SEVEN

The Clockwise Walk

ONE OF THE SATISFYING BYPRODUCTS OF FOCUSING ON THE three triads is that it provides a clearer starting point for exploring overall applications of the Third Approach. One has only three rather than nine differentiations to make.

There are both internal and external applications of the theory. The former refers to internal self-understanding and coming to balance. The latter refers to understanding and dealing with others. By way of an introduction to the applications, let me introduce the concept of the Clockwise Walk.

To do this, let us focus on one aspect of the Enneagram symbol, the circle. Using Figure 5 as a guide, try to visualize the circle as a large circular walkway accessible to each of the three triads. And just as it is much easier or more natural for us to walk forward rather than back-

Figure 5
The Clockwise Walk

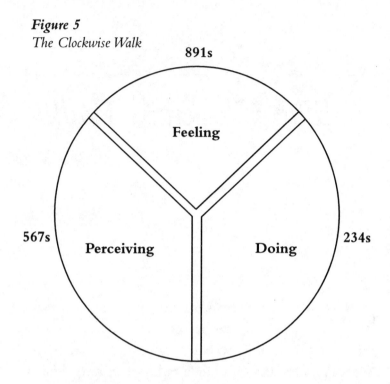

ward, I hypothesize a natural clockwise movement around the Enneagram circle. Moving clockwise around the Enneagram circle makes intuitive sense since the numbers depicting the nine types are arranged around the circle in clockwise order. Keeping in mind that moving forward is easier than moving backward, let us now apply the Clockwise Walk to the three triads and their Instinctive, Auxiliary, and Buried Functions.

The Internal Clockwise Walk: Capitalizing on our Auxiliary Function

As first discussed in Chapter 2, each triad has its own Instinctive, Auxiliary, and Buried Function. It will be helpful to illustrate these three functions once again.

Let us start each triad on its Clockwise Walk. 234s instinctively do things and then "naturally" try to perceive the responses of others to what they have done. 567s instinctively perceive data from the outside and then "naturally" feel strongly about what they have taken in. People in the 891 triad instinctively feel strongly about something and then "naturally" move to action.

The dynamics of the Clockwise Walk are as follows. The Instinctive Function of each triad, that function with which people in that triad are very familiar, is the starting point for their clockwise walk. The next natural step is toward each triad's Auxiliary Function, which is the bridge to their Buried Function.

Chart 7

Instinctive, Auxiliary, and Buried Functions

Triad	Instinctive Function	Auxiliary Function	Buried Function
234s	Doing	Perceiving	Feeling
567s	Perceiving	Feeling	Doing
891s	Feeling	Doing	Perceiving

Figure 6
The Clockwise Walk for 234s

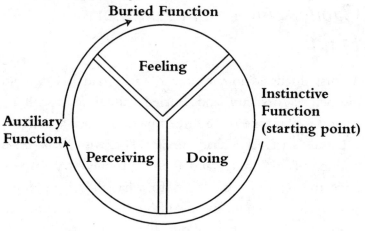

For 234s, Perceiving moves them from Doing to real Feelings (see Figure 6). Once 234s "let go" into Perceiving, they begin to be more comfortable with their Buried Function: Feeling. The lag between feeling *arising* and feeling *experienced* becomes shorter and shorter.

Once 567s "let go" into Feeling, they become energized to move from Perceiving to Doing (see Figure 7). Imagine 567s considering purchasing a new car, narrowing their options down to three, and then developing a list of reasons for and against purchasing each car. The only way they can make a decision and take action is by touching into Feeling. They must simply ask themselves: "Which of the three cars would I really *like* to have?" Once integrated with the data, Feeling prompts 567s into their Buried Function: Doing.

Doing something helps 891s move from Feeling to Perceiving (see Figure 8). This is how they gain perspec-

Figure 7
The Clockwise Walk for 567s

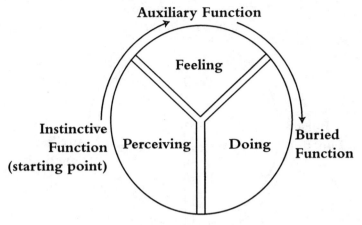

tive. Remember the advice to "count to ten" when angry? Counting to ten is *doing something.* Once 891s reach the count of ten, they may achieve something they did not have when the anger first arose: perspective. Ten seconds later the situation may look very different than it did at first! In other words, for 891s to get distance from their strong feelings, they need to do something to help them "let go" of being stuck in their feeling-of-the-moment. This could be nothing more than taking a walk. As a result, they can touch into their Buried Function: Perceiving. This gives them the perspective they need to separate from their feeling-of-the-moment.

The result of touching into our Buried Functions by way of our Auxiliary Functions is wholeness and balance. Wholeness or balance, for any of us in any triad, is possible only if we are willing to let go. We must learn to release the comfortable grip we have on our Instinctive

Figure 8
The Clockwise Walk for 891s

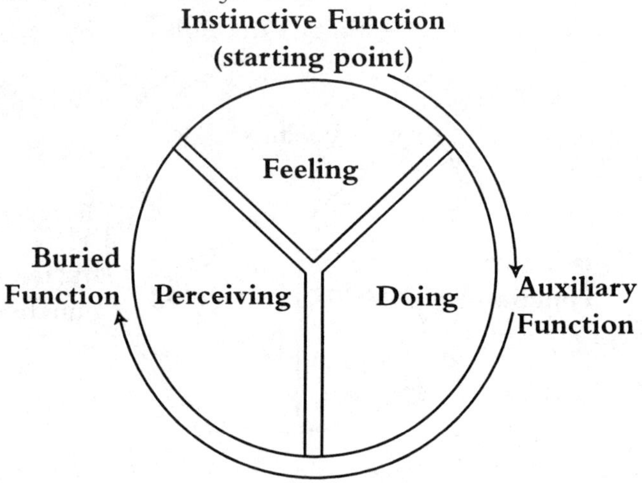

Instinctive Function
(starting point)

Feeling

Buried
Function Perceiving Doing **Auxiliary**
Function

Functions and allow our Auxiliary Functions to introduce us to our Buried Functions. This process of letting
go is reinforced gradually as we become more aware of
our natural dynamics. Since we do not change our type
or our triad, our Instinctive Function will always be on
alert, insisting on being our *exclusive* guide through every
situation. Self-awareness can lead us to a key insight at the
very moment our Instinctive Function yet again tries to
serve as our exclusive guide: "Ah, there I go again!" The
more self-aware I am, the sooner that insight will come.
And with that insight the change process begins. We
become more and more willing and able to let go of our
Instinctive Functions and to touch into our Auxiliary and
Buried Functions.

Animating the Clockwise Walk: The Wizard of Oz Revisited

The three functions can be clearly and usefully portrayed by linking them to the three characters Dorothy met in *The Wizard of Oz*.[1] I believe Sister Mary Helen Kelley was the first to write about this story in relationship to the Enneagram.[2] However, in the context of the Third Approach, let me present *The Wizard of Oz* in a way that I hope will bring out the relationship of the three Universal Functions as "lived" by each of the three characters Dorothy encountered.

The Tin Man represents the 234s. Can you imagine how excruciating it was for him (as a 234 for whom "doing" comes naturally) to be in the situation which Dorothy and the Scarecrow found him: *unable to move!* "Take the oil can," he said, "and oil my arms and legs so I can be *useful* again." The Tin Man, so strong on the *outside* in his ability to move and do and achieve, but hollow inside. He looked for a remedy and assistance from outside, not from within.

The Cowardly Lion represents the 567s, very in touch with fear. Attempting to portray what he knew was his role among the forest creatures, he could not even say "I am the king of the forest" without scaring himself!

The 891s are represented by the Scarecrow who, until Dorothy freed him, had spent his whole life in one field. The Scarecrow, made of straw, was most aware of his vulnerabilities, specifically his fear of burning. Because he identified so closely with his body, he was aware of what harm could befall him at any moment.

Each of the three characters was *looking for something,* symbolically representing, I suggest, their Buried Functions. The Tin Man was looking for a heart, the symbol of feeling. The Cowardly Lion was looking for courage. The Scarecrow was looking for a brain.

How did each of the three find their Buried Functions? The Tin Man, while immobile, apparently had time to *reflect.* Not being able to do anything on the "outside" gave him the opportunity to do some work on the "inside." He concluded that his life, focused as it had been on Doing, left a void. He was looking for the heart that would fill his hollow insides. Having this time to reflect, his Auxiliary Function of Perception led him to his Buried Function of Feeling. He indeed found his heart.

The Cowardly Lion got in touch with his Buried Function (Doing) by tapping into his Auxiliary Function (Feeling). Once he got in touch with his feelings for Dorothy, he could do what he realized needed to be done: save Dorothy from the burning building. In the process he found his courage. After all, isn't that what courage is, doing something in spite of being afraid? Neither doing without being afraid nor being afraid without doing can be called courage.

The Scarecrow got in touch with his Buried Function (Perception) by doing. What did he do? He took a walk with Dorothy, leaving his home field behind! His footing was wobbly at first, one of the very difficult experiences for 891s—to go someplace where there is no sure footing. By doing something (his Auxiliary Function) he gained the perspective that there was a whole world out there he never had seen.

Thus each of the three characters, in their own way, achieved wholeness by getting in touch with their Buried Function through their Auxiliary Function. They each took the Clockwise Walk.

The External Clockwise Walk: Who Understands Whom?

The external implication of the Clockwise Walk involves the answers to three questions: *"Whom do I understand best?" "Whom do I understand next best?"* and *"Whom do I understand least?"* I suggest that the people we understand the best are the people in our own triad. 891s understand 891s best, 234s understand 234s best, and 567s understand 567s best. It is, for example, common experience in business that, everything else being equal, managers tend to hire people just like themselves. Study after study has demonstrated that in a very short period, perhaps the half hour or so of interview time, we are able to establish a rapport with those who are just like us.

I suggest that the people we understand next best are those found in the triad ahead of us: 891s understand 234s next best, 234s understand 567s, and 567s understand 891s next best. It is almost as if in walking toward the triad in front of us we are able to "see" the character-

istics of that triad. These characteristics, of course, corre-
spond to our Auxiliary Functions.

Who are the people we understand least? I suggest
these are the people in the triad behind us. 891s tend to
understand 567s least, 567s do not understand 234s, and
234s are baffled by 891s. Remember, these are the people
in back of us, unseen, and therefore not understood. This
phenomenon, it seems to me, is the external equivalent of
the internal Buried Function of each of the triads.

It is true that 2s with a 1 wing, 5s with a 4 wing, and
8s with a 7 wing have a presence in the triad behind
them.[3] Thus it is probably the case that these Enneagram
types have more understanding of the triad behind them
than do the other two types in their triad. However, the
general principle of not understanding the triad behind
you, I believe, is still valid. I base this on the clockwise
dynamic of moving away from the characteristics of the
triad behind you and embracing the characteristics of
your own triad. In Chapter 8 I take this up at greater
length in discussing the attributes of what I call the
"obvious" position in each triad, that of the 258s.

Notice we are not talking about who tends to *like*
whom but rather who tends to *understand* whom.
Whether we like or dislike someone is based on so many
factors that it is difficult to try to isolate general inclina-
tions. There are some types—for instance, the aggressive
types, 378s—who may not at all like other 378s for the
very reason that they are in competition with them (3s),
have opposing outlooks (7s), or have more power (8s).
On the other hand, the compliant types, 126s, may very

well like other 126s precisely because of the similarity of their ability to surrender themselves to a person or an ideal. Withdrawn types, 459s, may like one another if they hold a similar outlook on life or may, because of jealousy (4s), difference in worldview (5s), or degree of tolerance for conflict (9s) tend to dislike one another.[4]

The significance of whom we do and do not understand is fascinating. If, for instance, you are married to or work with someone in the triad behind you, that person may understand more about you than you do about him or her. And if you tend not to be introspective, that same person may understand you better than you understand yourself!

CHAPTER EIGHT

The Three Triad Positions

ONE OF THE IMPLICATIONS OF THE CLOCKWISE WALK HAS to do with the dynamics of the three triad positions. There is a commonality between each of the three types in the same position, first, second, or third, in each of the three triads.[1] 2s, 5s, and 8s are in the first position of each triad; 3s, 6s, and 9s in the second position; and 1s, 4s, and 7s are in the third position.

Let us explore these positions in some detail, keeping in mind the natural movement of the Clockwise Walk. The first position in each triad introduces us to a new stance toward life. 2s, 5s, and 8s represent and incorporate all the dynamics of their triad. They are so true to form that they tend to be much more obvious about their life stance than people in the second and third positions. Thus I call the 2s, 5s, and 8s the *obvious*. This takes two forms, both internal and external. 258s are so close to and conscious of the dynamics of their own triad, having just "walked away" clockwise from the dynamics of the triad behind them. It is true that one of their wings, the 1 wing for the 2s, the 4 wing for the 5s, and the 7 wing for the 8s, keeps them attached to the triad behind them. However, 258s find themselves in the position of *introducing* a new life stance, that of their "resident" triad, and as a result obviously focus their energy more sharply on the instinct of their triad: "doing" for 2s, "perceiving" for 5s, and "feeling" for 8s. So fresh and new to them is the instinct of their "resident" triad that they put a great deal more effort into it than into the dynamics of the wing behind them. 258s tend to assume more than anyone else that others are just like them.

Secondly, as observed by others, 258s more obviously demonstrate the Doing, Perceiving, and Feeling of the three respective triads. They have a stronger, clearer expression of these functions than their triad counterparts. This is so, I believe, because their outer-directed focus of attention causes them to screen everyone and everything they encounter as either someone needing their help (2s), someone or something not fully known (5s), or someone who may try to oppress (8s).

Those in the second position, the 3s, 6s, and 9s, I call the *immersed*. These three types are called the "primary personality types" by Riso.[2] Palmer refers to them as the "three core points of the inner triangle."[3] Their wing or wings keep them locked within their triads. Of all the types, 369s are the least aware of their own dynamics, more on "automatic pilot," precisely because they are so immersed. *So much* of their energy goes into the dynamics of their triad.

Via their wings, 369s access all three variations of the theme within their resident triad. 3s can adapt to *anything,* having the ability to choose between being needed (their 2 wing), being useful (their own dynamic), being appropriate (their 4 wing), or being all three at the same time! 6s are situated between their 5 wing, which observes literally and painstakingly from afar, and their 7 wing, which observes instantaneously and experientially. As a result, 6s experience in their minds the literal naivete of the 5 and the endless possibilities of the 7. Driven by fear, they skeptically appraise whether what they observe is truly what it seems to be. 9s, positioned between two very outwardly impassioned types, see both 8s and 1s as on the brink of losing control. In their variation on the theme of "making justice," 9s can defend their own against an oppressor (their 8 wing) or can righteously point out the flaw (their 1 wing). They prefer to "cool their jets," staying calm on the outside while simultaneously expending effort to keep their deep feelings from sweeping them away.

I call 1s, 4s, and 7s, in the third position of each triad, the *divided.* It is as if the dynamics of each triad, though very much present, are already beginning to recede in this third position. At the same time, the dynamics of the next triad clockwise are already taking hold. The Clockwise Walk seems to be urging 147s to taste what is ahead. And so 147s find themselves in an "Am I here or there?"

stance, balancing between their own triad and the lure of the triad immediately in front of them. 147s have a *double instinct*. The first, of course, is the instinct of their own triad. The second follows immediately, is different and sometimes opposite. It is the instinct coming from the triad ahead of them. 147s struggle to accept the fact that within them there are two sometimes conflicting instincts which can pull them in two very different directions.

Thus 4s, like the other types in the "Doing" triad, instinctively move toward the outer environment. At the same time, 4s experience the 567 instinct of holding back, hesitating in order to find meaning in their flurry of activity, which is "life" to them. Hesitation also alerts 4s not to be so gauche in their outward movements.

7s, like their counterparts in the "Perceiving" triad, instinctively hold back to gain perspective. But at the very moment they do this 7s tap into the energy reserve of the 891s, particularly that of the 8s. This energy prompts the 7s to want to experience everything they can no matter how fearful they may be of what they are about to experience. This twofold dynamic of the 7s is best caught in the opening sentiments of the title song from the play *Cabaret,* "Don't sit and ponder alone in your room, come hear the music play...."[4] The instinct of 7s to come inside is countered by an opposite instinct that holds them back from getting too far inside where pain and discord may be lurking. 7s strive to "get out of their rooms," their heads, into pleasant experiences.

1s, like their counterparts in the "Feeling" triad, experience strong passions felt deeply. Yet at the same moment, they are pulled into the 234 triad, particularly into the "helpfulness" and "goodness" of the 2s. *"Good people don't get angry so, of course, I am not angry. I am just trying to make things better for everyone's good."* Thus 1s are prompted to "tidy up" themselves as well as the world around them. 1s walk through life with an eraser, attempting to eliminate the flaws.

147s strive for the "more" which it seems they hope to find in the dynamics of the triad ahead of them. The "more," they believe, will come sometime in the future: more perfection for the 1s, more harmony for the 4s, even more possibilities for the 7s.

> There is a striving after a canon of perfection: the good for the 1s, the beautiful for the 4s, the true for the 7s. If this canon is not met, then they strive for these. The striving involves CRAFTING of the good, the beautiful, the true. They make efforts to make things good, beautiful, true.[5]

Even though 147s embody the dynamics of their own triad, their divided stance causes them to express these dynamics in a way subtly different from their triad counterparts. This is yet another reminder, as we discussed in Chapter 3, that we each experience life through our own organismic filter.

CHAPTER NINE

Relating to People in the Triads

ANOTHER APPLICATION OF THE CLOCKWISE WALK HAS TO do with how we might effectively relate with other people. In relating to others, it is important to consider two questions: first, *"What is my reaction to them?"* and second, *"How can I best respond to them?"* In terms of the first question, it is all too easy to judge what we like and do not like about another. The more we dwell on this like/dislike dynamic, the further we might distance ourselves from the other.

Particularly when we have a negative reaction to another person, I believe it is imperative to ask ourselves a key question: "What is there about *me* that causes me to react to you the way I do?" This question puts an entirely new light on the situation. Instead of starting to list the characteristics we do not like about the other person, we begin our reflection by taking stock of *ourselves*. 234s may judge another as "inefficient" or "shabby" simply because efficiency and image are important to 234s. 567s may judge another as "invasive" or "thoughtless" simply because holding back and thinking things through are important to 567s. 891s may judge others as "fence straddling" or "pragmatic" simply because knowing where they stand and acting on values are important to 891s.

That brings us to the second question, how best to respond to others. In relating to others, it is important to keep in mind the distinction between what we are *comfortable with* (what comes "naturally"), and what is likely to be *effective* in the situation. In order to be effective, we may need to do something that is not so comfortable. To be effective in dealing with others, we need to keep their point of view and way of dealing with life in mind. To simply act out of our "comfort zone" may be natural for us. But it may not achieve the effect we intend with someone else. This is particularly true when that someone is in a different triad.

Discovering what will be effective is one application of using our Auxiliary Functions to get us in touch with our Buried Functions. It may very well be one of those two functions, rather than our Instinctive Function, that will provide the key to dealing effectively with the person or situation we face at the moment.

While considering how best to assist someone in a different triad, keep in mind the power of the Clockwise Walk. It may be that we have something to offer those in the triad ahead of us. What comes instinctively to us is precisely what is the Buried Function of those in the triad ahead of us. By the same logic, we have something to learn from the triad behind us. Our Buried Function is the Instinctive Function of the triad behind us. With this in mind, let us discuss some key strategies for relating to people in each of the three triads.

Relating to 234s

Remember that 234s are watching closely for cues and clues from you as to how they are doing. Be willing to give them an indication of where they stand with you. Reinforce positive behavior. Give them a chance to point out their own negative behavior; if they do not do so, then point it out to them. Otherwise they will probably think they are doing just what you want. Be forthright with them without being blunt. Say things directly, not obliquely; otherwise they may not realize you are talking about them.

234s tend to take things personally. It is important, particularly if you need to confront them, that you distinguish between the issue and the person. If you do not, 234s will think you are attacking them personally and thus may lose sight of the issue. Do not hesitate to confront, if necessary, but be sure to separate verbally what they did from who they are.

Remember that they are quick to say "yes" to whatever you have said or asked. Be sure they have not over-committed themselves, and be ready to challenge any unrealistic commitments they make. Realize that their connection to you and others is very important and that they fear losing that connection. Fear of losing the connection is often what prompts 234s not to confront others or not to display the anger they may be feeling. Hesitant to disagree because they may lose their connection with you, 234s tend not to disagree; this is their way of avoiding direct confrontation. Let them know that you expect them to be honest with you and that you neither want nor expect them to agree with everything you say.

Be aware that 234s need to feel good about their roles and image. Let them know they are an integral part of the group. If you need to "step on their image," try to do so in a humorous fashion, helping them to join you in puncturing their inflated "image balloon."

Do not take their self confidence at face value. Realize that there is probably a fair amount of insecurity underneath the "I've got it all together" image of competence. Be willing to accept a certain amount of boasting on their part; recounting their accomplishments is their way of compensating for their inner insecurity.

Help them understand that they cannot always secure their environment: things are sometimes very messy and open-ended; projects may need to be put on hold; there may not be a clear goal in sight.

When they become silent during a conversation, do not interrupt. It is likely they are reflecting on what was just said and need a moment to get perspective. It may be that they are getting in touch with affect and need a moment to "let themselves feel." Interrupting the silence will merely call them back to the arena where they are instinctively on center stage and may lose their opportunity to reach insight or touch into feeling. It is also possible that their silence is an attempt to hide a "negative" about themselves so that you will not think badly of them. In any case, after a few moments you might simply acknowledge the silence and ask them if they have any comment.

Relating to 567s

Remember that 567s will tend to hold back in looking for the overview, particularly when first dealing with you. They are not sure what your reaction will be to what they say: will you discount, make fun of, or misuse their thoughts? They simply do not know at first whether to trust you. And trust is one of their big issues. They need time to observe you in action, particularly noting whether you are as good as your word, before they will give you their trust. Their trust has to be earned; it is not a given. Realize they are and have been screening you all along. In their own good time, they will decide whether you can be trusted.

Even though they may not want to impose themselves on you and may tend to stay in the background, do not overlook or ignore them. If you do, their nagging fear of being discounted by others will surface. Rather, gently invite them to speak or to elaborate on their briefly stated, impetuous, or cryptic comments. Do not ridicule their ideas. Point out your view of the topic they just brought up, or at the very least comment on how you never have thought of it that way before. 567s are open to collecting different viewpoints, which they will test against their already processed data.

Respect their need for privacy. Reinforce any efforts they make to come out of themselves, but stay objective and matter-of-fact. Do not get into personal issues by asking them questions about themselves or their families. They may offer this information sometime down the line if and when they feel comfortable with you. But any attempt to get at personal information will be perceived as invasive prying on your part.

Do not get hooked into being their authority by giving them solutions. Rather, present alternatives for their consideration, letting them think out the matter for themselves and come to their own conclusions. Even if you were to offer a solution, chances are they would resist it!

Understand that 567s have difficulty making decisions because they feel they may not yet have collected enough data. Or they may resist making a decision which will in effect eliminate all but one of their treasured options. It may be appropriate for you to help them face making a decision by assisting them in tapping into their feelings. For example, ask them which alternative they would really *like* to choose!

Help 567s focus on the concrete and specific in order to get them beyond abstract ideas. Encourage them in making practical applications of their ideas. Help them to articulate novel ideas or possible solutions, even if at first the ideas seem ridiculous to them. It may be that their idea is the very thing that can move a discussion or project forward.

Remember that 567s tend to question everything. Be prepared to respond to their questions, but also anticipate their questions by posing questions yourself. This assures them that you are examining the issue or at least that you understand their thinking.

Relating to 891s

State things to 891s matter-of-factly; do not make a big deal of what you are saying. This includes praising as well as reprimanding. The bigger the deal you make, the less effective you will be with 891s. Do not tell them forcefully or repeatedly what you want; the less you make it a big deal, the more likely they will respond. 891s do things at their own pace and in their own good time. If you can live with that, fine. If not, confront them and be prepared to handle the moment of unpleasantness you may face in the confrontation.

Show 891s that you have the strength and willingness to stand up to them or at least to stand up for what you think is right. If you think you are right, do not give in, back off, or apologize. They will perceive you as "wishy-washy" or "whining" and therefore weak. You will earn their respect by standing your own ground with them.

Remember that boundaries are important to 891s. Respect their turf, whether physical or psychic. By the same token, confront 891s on their first intrusion into your own turf, thus exhibiting the strength that earns their respect. Be direct and candid in dealing with them and speak from your own beliefs, not from absolutes or rules or on behalf of others. 891s respect your right to *your own* thoughts and feelings even though they may not agree with you.

Do not directly challenge their strongly held feelings or standards. You will never win a direct argument with them. The battleground is part of *their* turf. Rather, try to get them to consider why others think differently. See if you can get them to make a case for the *opposite* view. You may not change their minds, at least not then and there, but you will have provided them the opportunity to get perspective by presenting another way of looking at things.

Remember, 891s always deal with issues, only sometimes with personalities. It is the issue at stake that is important to them and that has prompted their sometimes sudden or prolonged eruption. Do not take it personally, especially if you are a 234! Try to deal dispassionately with their logic. The only way you will be effective is by addressing step-by-step the points they have raised. Stick to the point. If you change the subject, they will suspect you really do not have a case. Be prepared for them to ventilate about their issue until their feelings have calmed down. Simply listening to them without comment is probably the best way to handle the eruption.

Above all, be fair, honest, and straightforward. Any hint of duplicity on your part will cause them to question your character. This will very likely turn them off to you and what you say. And once they have turned you off, it will be very difficult for you to regain their respect.

Afterword

As I have indicated, it is more natural to identify our triad before trying to sort through the nine Enneagram types. How much any of this rings true is, of course, up to you to decide. Whether you are new to or conversant with the Enneagram, your personal litmus test for the veracity of any of this is your own experience carefully reflected upon with an open mind. In that spirit, if any of this book rings true to you as it does to me, I hope it has given you insight into the dynamics of your "resident triad." I hope it has provided you an affirmation of the strengths and an awareness of the compulsions, both of which form the intricate fabric of your life. I hope it has provided you with a deeper understanding of the other triads and a greater appreciation for the profound differences present in the human experience. My best wishes to you as you take the next step on your Enneagram journey!

Notes

Acknowledgements

1. Suzanne Zuercher and Dick Wright, *Enneagram Cards* Notre Dame, IN: Ave Maria Press, 1994.

Introduction

1. Marika Dentai, in her recent article, "Instinctual Types: Self Preserving, Social and Sexual," *Enneagram Monthly* 1, no. 7 (September 1995), 1, 22-3, makes a convincing case for an even more basic starting point. She calls the instinctual type, by which our lives are dominated by that fundamental instinct by which we are *least in touch with our essence,* our "first differentiation" of personality. Utilizing Dentai's terminology, our Enneagram triad would thus become the "second differentiation" of our personality. Unlike our instinctive type, however, our triad is based on the Universal Function *most accessible* to us. Our Enneagram type would be the "third and most complex differentiation."

2. There are notable exceptions to this. Loretta Brady, in her book *Beginning Your Enneagram Journey* (Allen, TX: Tabor Publishing, 1994), devotes two entire chapters to the three

"centers." Kathleen Hurley and Theodore Dobson in *What's My Type?* and *My Best Self* (HarperSanFrancisco, 1991 & 1993) devote one chapter each. In *The Enneagram: A Journey of Self Discovery*, (Denville, N. J.: Dimension Books, Inc., 1984), Maria Beesing, et al., spend a third of a chapter on the "Types according to their Preferred Center"

Chapter 1

1. Helen Palmer, *The Enneagram* (San Francisco: Harper & Row, 1988), 9.

2. Ibid., 55.

3. Don Richard Riso, *Understanding the Enneagram: The Practical Guide to Personality Types* (Boston: Houghton Mifflin Company, 1990), 26.

4. Don Richard Riso, *Personality Types: Using the Enneagram for Self Discovery* (Boston: Houghton Mifflin Company, 1987), 24–26. Brackets mine.

5. Suzanne Zuercher, O.S.B., utilizes this third approach in her two books, *Enneagram Spirituality* and *Enneagram Companions* (Notre Dame, IN: Ave Maria Press, 1992 and 1993). Suzanne worked closely with Paul V. Robb, S.J., who himself began teaching the Enneagram in 1975. In 1976 Suzanne joined Paul as co-director of the Institute for Spiritual Leadership in Chicago. Through the mid-eighties, in that think-tank environment, they continued to develop and expand their understanding of the Enneagram, integrating this Third Approach into the year-long curriculum presented to each new class of 30–35 men and women who came from five continents.

6. Don Richard Riso, *Understanding the Enneagram*, 15.

7. "Gurdjieff's most original contribution to the enneagram teaching was in regard to the three centers [triads]. He taught that we are actually 'three-brained beings.' What is meant by this is that we each have three centers of intelligence, three

faculties through which we can know ourselves, others and the world." (Loretta Brady, *Beginning Your Enneagram Journey*, 33. Brackets mine.)

8. Kathleen Riordan Speeth, "The Gurdjieff Work," in Charles Tart, *Transpersonal Psychologies* (New York: Harper & Row, 1975), 286-7. Italics mine.

9. Many of Gurdjieff's thoughts are articulated in Ouspensky's book, *In Search of the Miraculous* (San Diego: Harcourt, Brace, Jovanovich, 1977).

10. Don Richard Riso, *Personality Types*, 1987), 13.

11. Kenneth Walker, *A Study of Gurdjieff's Teaching* (London: Jonathan Cape, 1957), 7.

12. Ibid., 14-5.

13. I will keep the term "man" throughout this historical narrative since that is the language said to have been used by Gurdjieff and Ouspensky.

14. Kenneth Walker, *A Study of Gurdjieff's Teaching*, 23-4.

15. Ibid., 24. Brackets mine.

16. Kathleen Riordan Speeth, "The Gurdjieff Work," in Charles Tart, *Transpersonal Psychologies*, 300-1. Brackets mine.

17. Kenneth Walker, *A Study of Gurdjieff's Teaching*, 24-5. Italics and brackets mine.

Chapter 2

1. Don Richard Riso, *Personality Types*, 1987), 26.

2. Kathleen Riordan Speeth, "The Gurdjieff Work," in Charles Tart, *Transpersonal Psychologies*, 286-7.

3. *Webster's New International Dictionary*, 3d. Ed., s.v. "feeling." I use the terms "feeling" and "emotion" interchangeably, following the dictionary definition of emotion as a "generalized or specific feeling."

4. Ibid., s.v. "sentiment."

5. *Webster's New World Dictionary*, College Edition, s.v. "do."

6. Kenneth Walker, *A Study of Gurdjieff's Teaching*, 24.

7. *Webster's New World Dictionary*, College Edition s.v. "perceive."

8. I am indebted to Suzanne Zuercher for introducing me to these three caricatures and for allowing me to incorporate them in this book. Suzanne utilized these caricatures in her basic Enneagram workshops.

9. Jolande Jacobi, *The Way of Individuation* (New York: New American Library, 1965), chapters 4 and 5.

Chapter 3

1. Excerpted from the unpublished notes of Paul V. Robb, S.J., titled "The Enneagram and Conversion," 1.

2. See Chapters 1, 2, and 10 of Suzanne Zuercher's *Enneagram Spirituality* for an insightful description of the movement from compulsion to balance by way of contemplation. Contemplation, as she explains it, is germane to people in all three triads.

3. Loretta Brady, *Beginning Your Enneagram Journey*, 39. Brackets mine.

4. Ibid., 45.

5. Ibid., 35. Brackets mine.

6. The gut as the true center is convincingly explained by Karl-fried Graf von Durckheim in *Hara: The Vital Centre of Man* (London: Allen and Unwin, 1985), in the chapter "The Order of Life in the Symbolism of the Body."

7. Kenneth Walker, *A Study of Gurdjieff's Teaching*, 24. Brackets mine.

8. Excerpted from the unpublished notes of Paul V. Robb, S.J., titled "The Enneagram and Conversion," 1.

9. The questions in this exercise were adapted from questions developed by Suzanne Zuercher. Some of them are based on questions Oscar Ichazo identified for each of the centers.

Chapter 4

1. Suzanne Zuercher, O.S.B., *Enneagram Spirituality*, 10. Italics mine.

Chapter 5

1. Helen Palmer, *The Enneagram*, 55.

2. I am most grateful to Loretta Brady, who in the course of several conversations provided me with considerable insight into these differences.

3. Loretta Brady, *Beginning Your Enneagram Journey*, 46. Brackets mine.

4. Suzanne Zuercher, O.S.B., *Enneagram Spirituality*, 11.

Chapter 6

1. Excerpted from the unpublished notes of Paul V. Robb, S.J., titled "The Enneagram and Conversion."

2. Billy Joel, "Shades of Grey," on *River of Dreams*, Sony Music Entertainment, Inc., 1993.

3. Suzanne Zuercher, O.S.B., *Enneagram Spirituality*, 13.

4. Cited in the unpublished Enneagram notes of Paul V. Robb, S.J.

5. Suzanne Zuercher, O.S.B., *Enneagram Spirituality*, 13.

6. Loretta Brady, *Beginning Your Enneagram Journey*, 38.

Chapter 7

1. L. Frank Baum, *The Wonderful Wizard of Oz*, first published 1900.

2. Sister Mary Helen Kelley, O.S.C., *Reality In Three Dimensions* (Memphis, TN: Monastery of St. Clare, 1992).

3. In Enneagram theory the concept of wing means the types immediately either side of your Enneagram type on the circle. A type 1, for instance, would have a nine and a two wing, a type 2 would have a one and a three wing, and so on. For our purposes here, think of your wings as secondary types.

4. Don Richard Riso used the descriptions Aggressive, Complaint, and Withdrawn to compare the Enneagram to Karen Horney's three "life solutions," the Expansive, the Self-Effacing, and the Resigned. (Don Richard Riso, *Personality Types*, 321-5.)

Chapter 8

1. I am indebted to Paul Robb, S.J., who termed the three traid positions "The Second Matrix." He has identified a total of four matrices by which each of the nine Enneagram types is related to each other type in a specific developmental sequence.

2. Don Richard Riso, *Personality Types*, 1987), 26.

3. Helen Palmer, *The Enneagram*, 69.

4. *Cabaret,* lyrics by Fred Ebb and music by John Kander (New York: Tams-Witmark, 1963).

5. Excerpted from the unpublished notes of Paul V. Robb, S.J., titled "1-4-7 Dynamics."

Index of Names

Index of Terms

Sources Utilized

Beesing, Maria, et al. *The Enneagram: A Journey of Self Discovery.* Denville, N. J.: Dimension Books, Inc., 1984.

Brady, Loretta, *Beginning Your Enneagram Journey.* Allen, TX: Tabor Publishing, 1994.

Hurley, Kathleen and Theodore Dobson. *What's My Type?* HarperSanFrancisco, 1991.

Jacobi, Jolande. *The Way of Individuation.* New York: New American Library, 1965.

Kelley, Sister Mary Helen, O. S. C. *Reality in Three Dimensions.* Memphis, TN: Monastery of St. Clare, 1992.

Ouspensky, P. D. *In Search of the Miraculous.* San Diego: Harcourt, Brace, Javonovich, 1977.

Palmer, Helen. *The Enneagram.* San Francisco: Harper & Row, 1988.

Riso, Don Richard. *Personality Types: Using the Enneagram for Self Discovery.* Boston: Houghton Mifflin Company, 1987.

Riso, Don Richard. *Understanding the Enneagram: The Practical Guide to Personality Types.* Boston: Houghton Mifflin Company, 1990.

Robb, Paul V. *Various unpublished Enneagram notes.*

Speeth, Kathleen Riordan. "The Gurdjieff Work." In *Transpersonal Psychologies,* ed. by Charles Tart. New York: Harper & Row, 1975.

von Duerckheim, Karlfried Graf. *Hara: The Vital Centre of Man.* London: Allen and Unwin, 1985.

Walker, Kenneth. *A Study of Gurdjieff's Teaching.* London: Jonathan Cape, 1957.

Zuercher, Suzanne. *Enneagram Companions.* Notre Dame: Ave Maria Press, 1993.

Zuercher, Suzanne. *Enneagram Spirituality.* Notre Dame: Ave Maria Press, 1992.

Zuercher, Suzanne and Dick Wright. *Enneagram Cards.* Notre Dame: Ave Maria Press, 1994.

About the Author

Dick Wright, Ph.D., has served in the organizational development field for over 20 years.

Prior to establishing **Wright Directions, Inc.** and co-founding **Elson/Wright Associates**, both management consulting firms, he was Corporate Director of Strategic Planning at Alexian Brothers Health System, Inc. and was Director of Management and Organizational Development at Loyola University of Chicago. He has also served as a high school teacher, guidance counselor, and administrator.

Dick has conducted hundreds of presentations and workshops throughout the country before top executives, board members, middle managers, supervisors, and support staff, and has undertaken a variety of consulting assignments primarily with not-for-profit service organizations. He has been a featured speaker at national conventions of the American College of Healthcare Executives, the American Medical Record Association, the American Society of Clinical Pathologists, the American Society of Ophthalmic Administrators, the American Society of Radiation Oncologists, the American Society of Training and Development, the Image Industry Council International, and the Learning Resource Network.

In 1989 Dick began to develop and teach a wide variety of personal development workshops, including introductory and advanced courses on the Enneagram Personality System. He currently serves on the continuing education faculties at College of Lake County in Grayslake, Illinois and McHenry County College in Crystal Lake, Illinois.

Dick was introduced to the Enneagram in 1989 by Suzanne Zuercher, O.S.B., who since the mid-70s has taught the Enneagram and has authored three books and a tape series on Enneagram applications. Dick has become an enthusiastic student, teacher, and writer on the Enneagram personality theory. Having studied under Helen Palmer, he has undertaken comprehensive training with Don Riso and Russ Hudson. Dick has also collaborated with Suzanne Zuercher on a unique approach to identifying one's Enneagram type, *The Enneagram Cards*, published in 1994. He conducts an ongoing series of workshops on the Enneagram at the Oasis Center in Chicago and regularly writes articles for the *Enneagram Monthly*. This is his first book on the Enneagram Triads.

Dick's academic credentials include a Doctorate in Educational Administration and Masters degrees in Guidance and Counseling and in Business Administration. His Bachelor's Degree is in Philosophy.